Prophets c

For Charles and Sally Allix

Also by Peter Mullen

Fiction
Blessed Assurance
Only A Lad
Growing Up With Sex and Death
Rural Rites
Country Matters
Holy and Unholy Ghosts
Haunted Lives
The Politically Correct Gospel
A Grain of Mustard Seed

Poems
Words and Worse
Scattered Showers

Non-fiction
Beginning Philosophy
Thinking About Religion
Working With Morality
Being Saved
The New Babel
Dreams That Come True
Reason to Believe
Death
Death be not Proud
A History of the Promenade Concerts
Shrines of Our Lady
Words from St Michael's
Holy Smoke: Tales of a City Rector
Everyday Thoughts
Minute Sermons
The Secular Terrorist
A Partial Vision: English Christianity & The Great Betrayal
The Politically-Incorrect Lexicon

Prophets
&
Visionaries:

Writers of Judgement

Peter Mullen

RoperPenberthy Publishing

ISBN 978 1 903905 84 5

Cover design by Zaccmedia
Typeset by Avocet Typeset, Somerton, Somerset
Printed and bound in the UK by PublishPoint
from KnowledgePoint Limited, Reading

CONTENTS

Introduction

The men who form the subjects of these chapters were among the greatest minds of their times and they were some of the finest writers of English of any age. Such qualifications would be sufficient in themselves to make these writers interesting topics for review but today there are additional, and perhaps even more important, reasons why we should attend closely to them. First, they all dealt with the deep and everlasting questions of human life and its purpose and they did so with profound insight, penetration and originality. Secondly, they were not merely examples of that class who are now referred to as *intellectuals*, and still less were they *academics* in the forensic sense which that word has gathered to itself.

They had *character* and their preoccupation with both perennial issues and contemporary affairs alike was existential, involving their whole being and personality. They were committed and heartfelt. And it was, more than intelligence and literary ability alone, this personal and emotional relationship with the matters which were the subject of their writings, which supplied the extra edge, the spark and the spirit, enabling them to become prophets and visionaries. They addressed the crises of their times and this makes them so pertinent to ours.

Intellectual brilliance and academic diligence can carry a writer a long way – the fictional archetype is George Eliot's Mr Casaubon and the real-life practitioners are such as Diderot and the Encyclopaedists – but in order to penetrate to the interior of any matter, to the soul of the thing, it is necessary, as it were, to *incarnate* oneself in it and thereby to *suffer* on its account. In this way all prophets and visionaries are imitators of Christ. It could not be otherwise. It is this close, emotional, personal and existential commitment which turns a writer's words into poetry, even where the writing is ostensibly prose. No one becomes a great stylist by application alone, no matter how assiduous. These writers are true poets in the sense that they are not just *doing* something, but they are *making* something. And what they make has an additional layer or depth of reality about it, as they seem almost to turn words into *things*. This is the sacramental aspect of poetic genius, a distinction which these writers possessed in huge measure.

Knowledge and understanding are not the result of fact-gathering. No amount of research by itself can produce insight. Rather, to know something is to enter into an intimate relationship with that thing and so it is no coincidence that the translators of the King James Bible offer the one word know both for understanding and sexual relations: And Adam knew Eve his wife; and she conceived... It is one thing to sit at one's desk in front of the encyclopaedia and note the lengths of the world's longest rivers or highest mountains; it is quite another thing to seek understanding through participating with all the intellectual and personal faculties and senses. The quest for knowledge involves one in putting oneself, as it were, at the disposal of the thing one wants to know. It is a form of reverence and of awe. Apprehension before comprehension. There is no understanding without standing under.

Ordinarily competent writers – most of us can hardly hope to aspire to more than this – produce ordinarily competent books. Dr Johnson confessed he could not persevere to the end with such books and that he was "inclined to toss them aside." An ordinarily competent writer will tell us things we did not know, but the experience of reading their works is not much better than reading an official report, a government white paper or a manual of instruction. But Ezra Pound insisted that "..the reader has a right from time to time to expect to be refreshed with shards of ecstasy."

The reader is so refreshed, and frequently, by the authors

under discussion here. These writers enter into the depths of their subject and interpret it for the reader, as it were, from the inside. And it is from their position as insiders that they derive their authority. It is what makes their words spellbinding. The prophet and the visionary speaks from beyond and so plants the spirit and character of the beyond in the mind of the reader. It does not seem to matter much whether the reader happens to agree with what the writer is saying. For example, I have little sympathy for the positivistic philosophy of David Hume, but then one comes across a paragraph such as this from his *Essay Concerning the Human Understanding:*

> "When we run over our libraries, persuaded of these principles. What havoc must we make? If we take in our hand any volume of divinity or school metaphysics, for instance, let us ask, *Does it contain any abstract reasoning concerning quantity or number? No. Does it contain any experimental reasoning concerning matter of fact and existence? No.* Commit it then to the flames: for it can contain nothing but sophistry and illusion."

I find Nietzsche even less sympathetic, but then this from his chapter on scholars of the Casaubon sort, in *Also Spake Zarathustra:*

> "Too long did my soul sit hungry at their table; I have not been schooled, as they have, to crack knowledge as one cracks nuts. They sit cool in the cool shade: they want to be mere spectators in everything and they take care not to sit where the sun burns upon the steps."

Of course, the prophets and visionaries who wrote the holy scriptures demonstrate their interior familiarity with the beyond most powerfully of all. That is precisely what makes holy scripture *holy.* And in the face of such power to communicate the beyond, even the word *inspiration* sounds inadequate and meagre:

"Is it nothing to you, all ye that pass by? Behold and see if there is any sorrow like unto my sorrow, which is done unto me, wherewith the Lord hath afflicted me in the day of his fierce anger." (*Lamentations 1: 12*)

Or – I am opening the bible pretty much at random:

"And he turned to the woman, and said unto Simon, *Seest thou this woman? I entered into thine house, thou gavest me no water for my feet: but she hath washed my feet with tears, and wiped them with the hairs of her head. Thou gavest me no kiss: but this woman since the time I came in hath not ceased to kiss my feet*" (*St Luke 8: 44–45*)

With authority, not as the Scribes.

But the spellbinding quality is not limited to the realm of high literature. Occasionally, the revelatory power can turn up in a few well-chosen – or even accidental – words. And how much of poetry and sublime prose has an accidental quality about it? I do not believe it can be manufactured or contrived. The visionary words are the by-product of the writer's acute and profound concentration. He devotes himself to the matter in hand and the words seem to slip out by themselves. One strikes the anvil and the sparks fly upwards.

How much control does the writer actually exercise over his production? The prophets of the Old Testament are known to have spoken out of frenzy or ecstasy – *ek stasis*, literally standing outside oneself. A close analysis of the prophetic texts reveals a technique by which the prophet would work himself up to an emotional pitch and then deliver his judgement. For example:

"I hate, I despise your feasts and I take no delight in your solemn assemblies. Take away from me the noise of your songs, to the melody of your harps I will not listen..."

This part of the prophetic utterance is the psychological build-up, the crescendo or *Scheltrede* and it culminates in the judgement word, *Drowort*

> "...but let justice flow down like waters, and righteousness like an ever-flowing stream." (Amos 5: 8–9)

When we open *The Waste Land* or read Collingwood's exquisitely expressed letter to Gilbert Ryle, or come across one of the dazzling short poems of Hulme, it is hard to suppress the comparison with great music – with, say, the beginning of Haydn's *The Creation* where the meandering tonality which is the representation of chaos abruptly bursts whole and clean with the key of C-major: *Let there be light!* Or the ravishing slow movement from Schubert's *String Quintet in C* – and the bit where he goes so slowly he almost stops the music altogether from heartbreak. Shards of ecstasy.

These great revelatory moments in literature (or music, for that matter) owe part of their success to their complete unity of form with content: the particular form of expression thoroughly involves – *incarnates* – its meaning

> "The complete consort dancing together" (*Little Gidding, Four Quartets* – T.S. Eliot)

My grandfather was a newsagent and, when I was a small boy, I often used to accompany him on his rounds. This was the beginning of my education. Once, as we walked through the damp and dilapidated streets of the worn out north of England suburb, grandfather was relating the history of the Second World War. His description of the Nazi-Soviet Pact, revoked by Hitler's invasion of Russia, struck me with an immediacy that is with me still:

> "Then Hitler stabbed Stalin in the back."

I knew at once that the phrase was not being meant literally, and I saw the long hand of the Fuhrer, stretching out from

Nazi Germany into Russia, and plunging a long knife into the heart of the land itself.

A visionary phrase can turn up anywhere: there is no better description of encroaching darkness over a cricket match than Ray Illingworth's, *indifferent light*.

We need to notice another quality of prophetic or visionary utterance, the supercharged speech of the great writers: their statements are not monochrome, one-dimensional; rather they have a rich, deeply-layered form. Anthony Burgess called this sort of writing *opaque* and he gave the example of James Joyce's *Ulysses* which he contrasted with the far less interesting *transparent* quality of an airport novel such as *Princess Daisy* by Judith Krantz. With the great writers it is not simply a case of their saying baldly that something is true, or such and such is the case: instead, what is characteristically said is susceptible of a great deal more unpacking. It is rarely a case of *"X" is true, so "Y" must be false"* – as it usually is in the plot of the airport novel or in the interdepartmental report – but rather of a many-sided statement. G.K. Chesterton, for instance, is very inclined to the creative use of paradox – a form which (paradoxically!) reveals by its very opaqueness.

> "Our neighbour, precisely because he may be anybody, is everybody. He is a symbol because he is an accident." (*Orthodoxy* – G.K. Chesterton)

Inspired, supercharged utterance is never merely *literally true*. And this is where the fundamentalist interpretation of scripture goes wrong in, say, the belief that each of the six days of creation was a period of twenty-four hours. Or consider this famous verse from *St Mark's Gospel* in which Jesus answers the High Priest's question,

> "Art thou the Christ, the Son of the Blessed?"

And Jesus replies,

"I am: and ye shall see the Son of Man sitting on the right hand of power and coming in the clouds of heaven." (*St Mark 14: 61–62*).

Whatever this means it does not refer to something that is going to happen up in the sky, like a thunderstorm. And we need to ask, *What is meant by the word* SEE *here?*

Visionary and prophetic writing is often penetratingly original in a way that is almost shocking. For example, R.G. Collingwood does not try to defend belief in the Trinity as a *spiritual* reality against the hard-headed empiricism of scientific method. Instead, he argues that science itself would not be possible without the metaphysics of the Trinity:

> "Aristotle failed in his metaphysical analysis; and his failure was not limited to himself alone; the metaphysical mistake which he made was a commonplace of Greek thought. And since metaphysics is inseparable, as regards success or failure, from ordinary thinking, this breakdown of Greek metaphysics implied a breakdown of Greek science..." (*An Essay in Metaphysics* – R.G. Collingwood)

Most of the foregoing has been concerned with style and character in writing, but of course style is inseparable from what is being said, As usual, C.H. Sisson puts this exactly when he tells us,

> "Unfortunately, the choice of words determines what is being said."

It is a notable feature in all the writers under discussion here that, when they speak, they are worth listening to because their concerns are large ones and they are our concerns too. Newman, for instance, as long ago as the 1830s saw that *the* political and social issue of the 19th century was the opposition between authority and the new dogma of progress – or, as he put it, *between Catholicism and liberalism*. It is still the issue almost two hundred years later; and it shows every sign of becoming even more critical. That is why Newman remains important: he is not a journalist or a popular historian of ideas dealing only in eye-catching ephemera. His penetration to the centre of matters that persist is what makes him both prophet and visionary.

The same goes for T.S. Eliot's insistence on the need to maintain classical and Christian culture against *the barbarians and their motorised caravans.* He saw exactly that, if Christian culture is allowed to go, then western society goes with it.

"Do you need to be told that such modest attainments as you can boast in the way of polite society will hardly survive the faith to which they owe their significance?" (*Choruses from the Rock* – T.S. Eliot)

Eliot wrote first about cultural decline in the 1920s and 1930s. One is inclined to say, *If he thought things were bad then, he should see us now!* In other words, the prophetic and visionary author of *The Waste Land* and *The Idea of a Christian Society* is not fading from our view with the passage of time: his words are more pertinent now than when he first uttered them.

There are any number of examples. Hulme's insistence on good writing as the only defence against the barbarism of most of what is written is hardly less needed in the era of trash journalism, the Internet and txt-spk than it was in his day. And our sentimental culture of *spirituality* and the *body, mind and spirit shelf* needs Chesterton to continue to warn us against disembodied spirituality – Hampstead Buddhism – which he correctly identifies as the eternal heresy of Gnosticism. Collingwood criticised the destructive positivism which took hold in the 1930s. Now although Logical Positivism is no longer practised as it was in those days, the positivistic error –of imagining one can reason without absolute presuppositions – is still a dominant force in our present discourse. Or one could mention Sisson's defence of the monarchy as providing *a decent set of political liberties*

– necessary now more than ever given all our airy talk about *universal rights.*

And does anyone doubt that Coleridge, in the words that follow, has identified that deepest spiritual-psychological crisis which is at the centre of our being?

"Art thou under the tyranny of sin – a slave to vicious habits – at enmity with God, and a skulking fugitive from thine own conscience? The best and most Christian-like pity thou canst show is to take pity on thine own soul. The best and most acceptable service thou canst render is to do justice and show mercy to thyself". (*Aids to Reflection* – S.T. Coleridge)

But enough of scene-setting. The prophets and visionaries should speak for themselves. For they still speak eloquently to us in our condition today.

Peter Mullen, Eastbourne, 2014

Chapter 1

Samuel Johnson (1709–1784)

A bookseller's son, Samuel Johnson was born in Lichfield, Staffordshire and reputedly read every volume in his father's shop. He was educated at Lichfield grammar school and Pembroke College, Oxford, leaving without taking his degree. For a short time he worked as a schoolmaster at Market Bosworth before moving to Birmingham where he began to write. When he was twenty-six he married the widow Elizabeth "Tetty" Porter who was twenty years his senior. Together they founded a school at Edial, near Lichfield and the most celebrated of their pupils was the future actor David Garrick. The school was forced to close by its financial losses and in 1737, accompanied by the young Garrick, Johnson determined to make his career in London.

One of his earliest works was the tragedy *Irene* which had to wait twelve years for its first production – by Garrick. Johnson earned a frugal living writing parliamentary reports for *The Gentleman's Magazine.* He also wrote a successful biography of the poet Richard Savage which was published in 1744, the year after Savage's death. And he earned money by cataloguing the huge library of the Earl of Oxford. In 1747 he issued his prospectus for *A Dictionary of the English Language*, bringing this massive labour to fruition in 1755.

Johnson wrote a long poem *The Vanity of Human Wishes*, the most perceptive and penetrating of his early works. Singlehandedly, he founded, wrote and edited a magazine containing mostly moral essays, *The Rambler* which ran for two hundred-and-eight issues in the early 1750s. His wife died in 1752 and Johnson declined into a depression from which he barely emerged for the rest of his life. Despite the publication of his *Dictionary,* he was still obliged to take on literary hack work, reviews and essays in such as *The Literary magazine, The Idler* and *The Universal Chronicle*. When his mother died in 1759, he wrote, in a single week, the long moral parable *Rasselas: The Prince of Abysinnia* in order to pay the funeral expenses.

In 1760 King George III awarded him a pension of £300pa for life and this was the first time he had enjoyed anything approaching financial security. In 1763 he struck up a deep and affectionate friendship with the young James Boswell who wrote Johnson's *Life*, perhaps the most famous of all literary biographies. In 1773 Johnson and Boswell embarked on a tour of the Hebrides described in *A Journey to the Western Isles of Scotland* (1775)

He founded The Literary Club – his famous talking shop, dining society and salon – whose members included the painter Joshua Reynolds, the historian, politician and polemical essayist Edmund Burke, Oliver Goldsmith, the playwright and the Liberal statesman Charles James Fox. Johnson published, in eight volumes, a critical edition of all the plays of Shakespeare and the ten volumes *Lives of the Most Eminent English Poets*.

In 1781 Johnson's long-term friend, the wealthy brewer Henry Thrale died. Thrale's widow Hester had looked after Johnson through periods of illness and when in 1784 she married the Italian musician Gabriele Piozzi, Johnson was distraught. He became deeply dejected and died before the end of the year.

Samuel Johnson is so voluminous, such a world in himself, that whole books have been written giving only the meanest caricature. So a single chapter is bound to be a foolish enterprise. I shall have to leave out so much that is fascinating and vital and concentrate on those parts of his huge being which were his lifetime obsessions: his psychology and his religion. In those things he applied his outstanding qualities of perception and insight relentlessly and to extraordinarily creative effect. But I should say a few things about other parts of his life and work first.

He seemed to have been born with the many discomforts

that were to last all his life. The milk of his wet nurse turned out to be tubercular. He was blind in his left eye and badly-sighted in the other one. He was deaf in his left ear and he caught smallpox. These things did not impede his literary career which began with his writing an epitaph for a duck he trod on when he was three. The wit – we might as well be honest and call it cheek – was there from the start: when his mother called him a puppy, he replied,

"And do you know what they call a puppy's mother?"

He had a large appetite and once at his aunt's he ate so much of a boiled leg of mutton that she talked about it for years. He was touched for his scrofula by Queen Anne. When he was in his sixties he said,

"My health has been from my twentieth year such as has seldom given me a single day of ease."

Everything about him was huge and voracious. Boswell said,

"I never knew any man who relished good eating more than he did. When at table he was totally absorbed in the business of the moment. His looks seemed riveted to his plate. Nor would he say one word or pay the least attention to what was said by others till he had satisfied his appetite, which was so fierce and indulged with such intenseness that, while in the act of eating, the veins on his forehead swelled and generally a strong perspiration was visible. To those whose sensations were delicate, this could not be but disgusting; and it was doubtless not very suitable to the character of a philosopher."

And though he could be rigidly abstemious, he was never temperate in either eating or drinking. He could refrain but he could not use moderately. He said of himself,

"I have no objection to a man's drinking wine, if he can

do it in moderation. I found myself apt to go in excess in it and therefore after having been some time without it on account of illness, I thought it better not to return to it. Every man is to judge for himself according to the effects which he experiences. One of the Fathers tells us he found fasting made him so peevish he did not practise it.

"I do not say it is wrong to produce self-complacency by drinking. I only deny that it improves the mind. When I drank wine, I scorned to drink it in company. I have drunk many a bottle by myself in the first place because I had need of it to raise my spirits; in the second place because I would have no man witness its effects upon me."

Sometime later Boswell said,

"He told me I might now have the pleasure to see him drink wine again, for he had lately returned to it. When I mentioned this to Johnson, he said, *I drink it now sometimes but not socially*. The first evening that I was with him at the Thrales, I observed he poured a quantity of it into a large glass and swallowed it greedily. Everything about his character and manners was forcible and violent. There was never any moderation."

He was also excessive and immoderate in his application to his literary labours and he could easily complete in a day a piece of work which might take an ordinarily competent man a whole week.

He lived for conversation and argument and said a seat in a tavern was the best place on earth. And although Boswell famously said to him after an evening's banter,

"You tossed and gored a great many, Sir" —

he also said,

"That he was occasionally remarkable for violence of temper may be granted: but let us ascertain the degree and not let it be supposed that he was in a perpetual rage and never without a club in his hand to knock down everyone who approached him. On the contrary, the truth is that by much the greatest part of his time he was civil, obliging, nay polite in the true sense of the word; so much so that many gentlemen who were long acquainted with him never received or even heard a severe expression from him".

Johnson said,

"It is a man's business to *command* his temper".

He had no taste for painting, though he and Joshua Reynolds were great friends, and Boswell says,

"He was very insensible to the power of music"

– a remark perhaps contradicted by Johnson himself when he confessed,

"Had I learnt to fiddle, I should have done nothing else".

As for his reputed uncouthness, Boswell tells us:

"Such was the heat and irritability of his blood that not only did he pare his nails to the quick, but scraped the joints of his fingers with a penknife till they were red and raw.

"His figure was large and well-formed and his countenance of the cast of an ancient statue; yet his appearance was rendered strange and somewhat uncouth by convulsive cramps, by the scars of that distemper which it was once imagined the Royal Touch could cure, and by a slovenly mode of dress. Though he had the use only of one eye, yet so much does mind govern and even supply the deficiency of organs that his visual perceptions, as far as they extended, were uncommonly quick and accurate. So morbid was his temperament that he never knew the joy of a free and vigorous use of his limbs: when he walked it was like the struggling gait of one in fetters; when he rode he had no command or direction of his horse, but was carried as if in a balloon. That with his constitution and habits of life he should have lived seventy-five years is a proof that an inherent vitality is a powerful preservative of the human frame.

"He would always be shaking his head and rolling himself about in a ridiculous manner."

Johnson was turned down for one teaching post because, as the headmaster said,

"He has such a way of distorting his face that it might affect some of the lads"

When he did spend some time teaching, his pupil and friend the actor David Garrick said,

"His oddities of manner and uncouth gesticulation could not but be the source of merriment to the boys. The young rogues used to listen at the door of his bedchamber and peep through the keyhole that they might turn into ridicule his tumultuous and awkward fondness for Mrs Johnson."

Tumultuous is an apt word for his behaviour. Once in the theatre he returned to find a man had taken his seat. He picked up the seat, with the man in it, and threw both man and seat into the pit. He loved rolling down grassy hills. On his tour of the Hebrides with Boswell, he jumped from the ship into the sea and swam the last part of the way to shore. And on being warned of a particularly dangerous pool, he jumped straight into it. His clothes were so ragged and his table manners so disturbing that sometimes when he was invited to meet some prominent person, he would conduct the interview while eating behind a screen.

He went to Oxford where he was very brilliant but had to leave without his degree when his money ran out. This experience threw him into a depression for several years and he did bits and pieces jobs and nothing, until setting off with Garrick for London, to try to make his way as a writer. For the journey they could afford only one horse and had to take turns. When they arrived in London, Johnson had tuppence-halfpenny and Garrick three-halfpence. He had married by this time – at St Werburgh's church, Derby on 9th July 1735 – but he left his wife behind with the intention of sending for her when he had established himself.

It was a strange marriage. He was twenty-five and his wife, Elizabeth Jervis Porter, was a widow aged forty-five with three teenage children. He called her Tetty and said,

"It was a love match on both sides"

Boswell says Tetty was

"...large, buxom and highly coloured".

But Garrick added to this portrait:

"She was very fat with a bosom of more than ordinary protruberance with swelled cheeks of a florid red produced by thick painting and increased by the liberal use of cordials; flaring and fantastic in her dress and affected both in her speech and general behaviour. Johnson's friend Hawkins said he'd married her because he couldn't see very well."

However, Tetty described Johnson as,

"...the most sensible man I ever saw."

She would stand up to him. Once, when he started to say Grace before the meal, she chastised him,

> "Nay hold, Mr Johnson: do not make a farce of thanking God for a dinner which in a few minutes you will protest not eatable!"

They did live together for a while but, as Walter Bate says in his excellent biography,

> "Between 1737 and 1739 something happened between him and Tetty and they began to live apart."

She began drinking heavily and turned to opium. She was hypochondriac and Johnson had to pay huge bills for treatments. She wouldn't leave the house and rather pathetically began to use even more rouge, saying she was disturbed by the difference in their ages. Johnson spent two-thirds of his meagre and unreliable freelance writer's income on her and, poor as they were, she always had a maid. Bate says that her various illnesses meant the end of sexual relations between them –

> "...despite a touching persistence on Johnson's part".

Tetty died in March 1752.

Johnson was acutely distressed and he felt guilty. He forever felt guilty, turning to God and praying,

> "Enable me to begin and perfect that reformation which I promised her."

It is difficult to know what sort of marriage they had. Johnson was a man of strong desires and there were rumours about his licentious behaviour as a young man. Boswell tells how,

> "...two young women from Staffordshire consulted him on the subject of Methodism. Johnson said to them,

*Come you pretty fools and dine with Maxwell and me at
The Mitre and we will talk over the subject* – which they
did. And after dinner he took one of them on his knee and
fondled her for half an hour."

Boswell, himself hardly a chaste young man, said,

"When Johnson was young it was well-known his amorous
inclinations were uncommonly strong and impetuous. He
owned to many of his friends that he used to take women
of the town to taverns."

Johnson was aware of his lustfulness and ashamed of it.
Refusing David Hume's invitation to sit in the green room at
the theatre, he said,

"I'll come no more behind your scenes, David. For the silk
stockings and white bosoms of your actresses excite my
amorous propensities."

He was preternaturally aware and intelligent. One might
say he had too much consciousness for his own good. His
memory was phenomenal. Once at Oxford a friend recited
to him eighteen Latin verses which he then repeated
verbatim, varying only one epithet – and that was to
improve the line. His attitude towards both reading and
writing was ambivalent. He would work intensively for
very long periods and then fall into prolonged idleness and
depression saying,

"I have read few books through. They are generally so
repulsive I cannot."

And he described scholarship, reviewing and writing generally as,

"...the epidemical conspiracy for the destruction of paper"

Making his way in London was hard. He wrote for magazines for small amounts of money but enjoyed his first success with a long poem called *London:*

"Here the fell attorney prowls for prey;
Here falling houses thunder on your head
And here a female atheist talks you dead."

He wrote up weekly the parliamentary debates – some half a million words altogether. The astonishing thing about his method was that he very largely invented the speeches from news reports. But his versions were so good that scholars and other commentators quoted from them for a century and many aspiring public speakers took them for their model.

Johnson was a moralist. He wrote *The Vanity of Human Wishes* when he was thirty-nine and the fantastic novel *Rasselas* nine years later. His edition of Shakespeare's works is vast and illuminating. He was not an academic but a seer, a sage and an imaginative genius who saw through to the heart of things; who, as it were, saw things from the inside. Here, for instance, among his many inventive remarks on Shakespeare:

"He who would illustrate Shakespeare by a quotation is like a man who, trying to sell his house, used to take round a brick from it in his pocket".

The King asked him to write the biography of English literature and he produced the magnificent *Lives of the Poets*. But it is for the *Dictionary* that he is universally regarded. He had assistants on this great work and typically paid them over the odds out of his kindness. And he accomplished it all in a tenth of the time it took the whole French Academy of forty scholars to produce their dictionary. Voltaire himself urged the French to follow Johnson's method. For this colossal labour, Johnson was paid £1575 in instalments.

He described himself as temperamentally unsuited to dictionary-writing: full of rebellious indolence and the desire to get any piece of work over quickly. In the *Dictionary* he defined *lexicographer* as,

"...a harmless drudge."

Once he was asked by two ladies why he came to define *pastern* as *the knee of a horse*. And he replied,

"Ignorance, ladies. Pure ignorance".

Another lady asked him why he had left out rude and obscene words and he said,

"I see you have been looking for them, Madam!"

When the *Dictionary* was published, the Earl of Chesterfield, under the description of *Patron* was brought in to write a commendation. This prompted one of the most brilliant short letters in English. Johnson wrote to Chesterfield:

"Is not a Patron, My Lord, one who looks with uncon-cern on a man struggling for his life in the water and, when he has reached ground, encumbers him with help? The notice which you have been pleased to take of my labours, had it been early, had been kind; but it has been delayed until I am indifferent and cannot enjoy it; till I am solitary and cannot impart it; till I am known and do not want it. I hope it is no very cynical asperity not to confess obligations where no benefit has been received, or to be unwilling that the public should consider me as owing to a Patron that which Providence has enabled me to do for myself."

Johnson is renowned as the archetypal Tory – and he was. He was not, that is, a free-market Liberal. Those were the Whigs whom Johnson described as *vile* and he said the first Whig was the devil. The Whigs were the party of great landowners and wealthy merchants. Tories were small landowners and country clergy and it was these whom Johnson preferred. He believed in small government, seeing all forms of administration as a necessary evil, constructed and managed as it was bound to be by fallible, sinful men. The whole of his political and literary judgement was based firmly on his psychological understanding, and this understanding was profoundly Christian: that is, he saw human beings as ineluctably tainted and marred by Original Sin, with the hope of redemption available only through the sacrifice of Jesus Christ. His radical interpretation of Christian morality made him an early opponent of slavery and Boswell tells us that when he was,

> "...in company with some very grave men in Oxford university, his toast was, *Here's to the next insurrection of the Negroes in the West Indies."*

He was a profound monarchist and he was once given an audience with the King. When Boswell asked him what they had talked about, Johnson replied,

> "It is not for me to bandy civilities with my Sovereign". As to the famous definition of *patriotism* as *the last refuge of a scoundrel*, Boswell says,

> "He did not mean a real and generous love of our country. He meant that pretended patriotism which so many have made a cloak for self-interest."

He hated republicanism and once when Dr Price defended this system in Oxford, Johnson noisily left the room. He despised the romantic politics of Rousseau and said,

> "Rousseau knows he is talking nonsense and laughs at the world for staring at him."

One day Sir Adam Ferguson said to him,

"Sir it is surely a good thing to keep up a spirit in the people as a balance against the Crown."

Johnson put him down:

"Sir, I perceive you are a vile Whig. Why all this childish jealousy of the Crown? The Crown has not power *enough*."

Again, it was his acceptance of the doctrine of Original Sin – and more than any merely doctrinal assent but as a painful sensation from which he scarcely escaped for a moment – which enabled him to see clearly the Whig belief in progress for the nonsense it was then and is today among those who are pleased to be regarded as *liberals*. He said,

"Whiggism is a laughable scheme of political improvement – no better than the politics of stock-jobbers and the religion of infidels."

He claimed,

"...a just abhorrence of Milton who had written in justification of the murder of his Sovereign...a man who never spared any asperity of reproach or brutality or insolence... an acrimonious and surly republican who in his domestic relations was so severe and arbitrary and whose head was filled with the hardest and most dismal texts of Calvinism."

All his life, Johnson was melancholic and often on the edge of despair. Sometimes he himself admits he was insane. This is because he was overstocked with consciousness, self-consciousness and God-consciousness. He would have made a good companion for Wittgenstein who used to go to the cinema and sit in the front row watching old black and white cowboy films to take his mind off the problems of philosophy which, for him, were indistinguishable from the problems arising from his own deep sense of sin, guilt and inadequacy. On one occasion Johnson was rescued by Mr and Mrs Thrale who came in to find him on his knees pathetically raving about madness and sin in front of a priest.

He spoke of,

> "...vile melancholy which has made me mad all my life".

And Boswell said the only book that would get him out of bed before noon was Burton's *Anatomy of Melancholy*. When he was in Lichfield he would frequently walk to Birmingham and back to escape *himself*. This was what he called *the great business of life* – to escape from himself. He said,

> "I have frequented the theatre more than in former seasons. But I have gone thither only to escape myself. I would have a limb amputated to recover my spirits".

And Angus Calder wrote that,

> "His profound affinity with Boswell derived from the fact that both men were guilt-ridden depressives."

But at the same time he knew that melancholy was useless and pointless: *Which of you by taking thought can add one cubit to his stature*. Worse he strongly believed that melancholy was sinful and he compounded his guilty feelings by feeling guilty about not feeling guilty enough. He fell into obsessive-compulsive actions, touching lampposts and counting his steps. He knew all this was wrong and a waste of life. He said so nearly every day and, being Samuel Johnson, he said it in vivid and powerful ways: once to Boswell,

> "I love every part of you except your affectation of distress."

And again:

> "You are always complaining of melancholy and I conclude

from those complaints that you are fond of it. No man talks of that which he is desirous to conceal and every man desires to conceal that of which he is ashamed. Make it an invariable and obligatory law never to mention your own mental diseases. If you are never to speak of them, you will think of them but little. And if you think little of them, they will molest you rarely. When you talk of them, it is plain that you want either praise or pity. For praise there is no room and pity will do you no good. Therefore, from this hour think no more about them. Sir, you have but two topics, yourself and me; and I am sick of both."

He said,

"It is wise to be serious, but it is useless and foolish – and perhaps sinful – to be gloomy."

But physician Johnson could not heal himself.
He said,

"Labouring men who work hard and live sparingly are seldom troubled with low spirits. If thou be solitary, be not idle. If thou be idle, be not solitary. Take a course of chemistry or rope-dancing: anything that will get the mind off itself. A man is happy never except when he is drunk."

And he counselled,

"It is best to throw life into a method, that every hour may bring its employment and every employment have its hour."

And,

"How much misery is escaped by frequent and violent agitation of the body!"

It was from Johnson that the frequently depressed Winston Churchill derived the phrase *the black dog.*

Though he would have despised psychoanalysis and our preoccupation with introspection and navel-gazing, he had great insight into his own psychology. He knew the disease and he knew the cure:

> "Do not hope wholly to reason away your troubles; do not feed them with attention and they will die imperceptibly away. Fix your thoughts upon your business, fill your intervals with company, and sunshine will again break in on your mind."

How his acute consciousness of his sinfulness would have caused him to scorn our fatuous cultivation of *self-esteem.* Oneself is the very thing one should not esteem.

And he believed that we are not finally the victims of our emotions but that will and act can alter our feelings and moods. This he got from St Augustine who urged *hypocrisy* as a practical virtue: pretend to something desirable until you make it real. Johnson likewise spoke of,

> "...the insidious power of habits, pictured as pigmies, that smooth one's path up the mountain of existence."

And our inner, mental state is not something airy and indefinable – something merely *spiritual.* As he said,

> "Intentions must be gathered from acts".

How he would have mocked today's therapeutic culture and the unhealthy and useless preoccupation with *spirituality.*

Jonathan Bate refers to,

> "...the severe rein he kept on any temptation to project outward and to blame external conditions."

Johnson would have hated our victim culture. He denied that we are victims of ourselves and said,

> "A man's being in good or bad humour depends on his will."

This is another insight which derives from St Augustine. God knows what epithet he would have coined for our psychologists and courts who describe murderers as *suffering from narcissistic personality disorder.*

At the centre of his politics was the monarch. At the centre of his whole psychological makeup and personality was God and the constant sense of God's presence like a haunting. Boswell said of him,

> "He was a sincere and zealous Christian of High Church of England and monarchical principles which he would not tamely suffer to be questioned."

All his life he ghosted sermons for parsons. But Boswell says,

> "He did not accept a Living because he was persuaded that his temper and habits rendered him unfit for that assiduous and familiar instruction of the vulgar and inno-cent which he held to be the duty of a clergyman."

He generally thought the clergy were a poor lot:

> "This merriment of parsons is mightily offensive."

And of the theological fads of the time,

> "Ancient ruffles and modern principles do not agree."

But he was not prissy and puritanical. In short, he was not Milton. Of a clergyman turned down for a benefice because five years earlier he had been found guilty of fornication, he said:

"Why Sir, he has repented. If a man is good enough to go to heaven, he is good enough to be a beneficed clergyman."

He was regular at church but remarked vehemently on what he too often found there:

"I am convinced that I ought to be present at divine service more frequently than I am; but the provocations given by ignorant and affected preachers too often disturb the mental calm which otherwise would succeed to prayer. I am apt to whisper to myself on such occasions, *How can this illiterate fellow dream of fixing attention after we have been listening to the sublimest truths conveyed in the most chaste and exalted language?*"

Johnson believed the Christian Creed fully and explicitly. He said,

"The mind can only repose itself on the stability of truth."

He did not share the fashionable 18th century sophistication and the tendency to regard religious doctrines as if they were metaphors for psychological states. He was once in a discussion and he turned morose. A lady asked him what was the matter and he said,

"I think I may be damned."

She said,

"What do you mean, Sir, to be damned?"
"Sent to hell and punished everlastingly."
"You seem, Sir, to forget the merits of our Redeemer."
"Madam, I do not forget the merits of our Redeemer. But our Redeemer has said that he will set some at his right hand and some at his left."

He disgusted himself. One Good Friday confession was simply:

> "I have made no reformation. I have lived totally useless, more sensual in thought, more addicted to wine and meat."

He did not have the easy-going attitude of his great friend Edmund Burke who said,

> "While I am honoured to be the Member of Parliament for Bristol, I should not like to live there. I would always have to be on my best behaviour!"

Johnson had a lifelong abhorrence of lying, even about the smallest matters. And of lying to save someone's feelings he said,

> "I deny the lawfulness of telling a lie to a sick man for fear of alarming him. You have no business with consequences: you are to tell the truth. Besides you are not sure what effect your telling him that he is in danger may have. It may bring his distemper to a crisis and that may cure him. Of all lying, I have the greatest abhorrence on this because I believe it has frequently been practised on me."

And he was so uncompromising about the stability of truth that today he would be dismissed as out of date, unwilling to accept the extreme relativism of post-modernity and obsession with *diversity.* Johnson was nothing if not robustly politically-incorrect.

As Boswell says,

> "He defended the Inquisition and maintained that false doctrine should be checked on its first appearance and that the civil power should unite with the church in punishing those who dared attack established religion."

When his aged mother consulted him with anxiety on the perplexing difficulties of the times, he advised her to keep to the old religion.

Johnson told Boswell,

"Let the blindness of the Mahometans confirm you in Christianity."

His words would earn a fatwa these days and, perhaps worse, the disapproval of the chattering classes

I am sure that the great many people who have a sentimental regard for Samuel Johnson as a composite of table-wit and Father Christmas would hate him if they knew more about him. A man of firm judgements, he would not thrive in our culture of *non-judgementalism.*

He said,

"I know of no good prayers except those in *The Book of Common Prayer*".

But he wrote hundreds of wonderfully heartfelt and tender prayers himself. For example:

"Give me grace to withdraw my mind from unprofitable and dangerous enquiries, from difficulties vainly curious and doubts impossible to be solved. Let me rejoice in the light which thou hast imparted. Let me serve thee with active zeal and humble confidence."

And he did serve. His Christianity was practical. Boswell says,

"He for years nursed whole nests of people in his house where the lame, the blind, the sick and the sorrowful found a sure retreat from all the evils whence his little income could secure them."

And Mrs Thrale said of him,

"His soul was not different from that of another person. It was simply greater."

And again Boswell says,

"He frequently gave all the silver in his pocket to the poor. Coming home one night he found a poor woman lying in the street, so much exhausted that she could not walk. He took her on his back and carried her to his house where he discovered that she was one of those wretched females who had fallen into the lowest state of vice, poverty and disease. Instead of harshly upbraiding her, he had her taken care of with all tenderness for a long time, at considerable expense, till she was restored to health; and endeavoured to put her into a virtuous way of living."

He lacerated any escape into sentimentality – especially in himself – with self-deprecating humour and wit, once complaining to Boswell about someone who had criticised him:

"He said that I sometimes contradicted people in conversation. Now what harm does it do to any man to be contradicted?"
"I suppose he meant the manner of it – doing it roughly and harshly."
"And who is the worse for that?"
"It hurts people of weak nerves."
"I know no such weak-nerved people."

Boswell said,

"I related this conversation to Burke who said, *It is well with a man who when he comes to die has nothing more on his conscience than having been a little rough in conversation'.*"

He was seventy-five when he died. As he approached the end he declared:

"I will be conquered. I will not capitulate. But I will take no more physic, not even my opiates. For I have prayed that I may render up my soul to God unclouded."

This was the man who had said to Boswell years before that,

"The fear of death is so much natural to a man that the whole of life is but a keeping away of the thoughts of it."

And Boswell said,

"I shall never forget the tremulous earnestness with which he pronounced the awful petition in The Litany, *In the hour of our death and at the Day of judgement, Good Lord, deliver us.*"

A few days before he died, Johnson received the Blessed Sacrament for the last time and composed this prayer:

"Almighty and most merciful Father, I am now as to human eyes it seems, about to commemorate for the last time the death of thy Son Jesus Christ our Saviour and Redeemer. Grant O Lord that my whole hope and confidence may be in his merits, and thy mercy enforce and accept my imperfect repentance. Make this commemoration available to the confirmation of my faith, the establishment of my hope and the enlargement of my charity. And make the death of thy Son Jesus Christ effectual to my redemption. Have mercy upon me and pardon the multitude of my offences. Bless my friends. Have mercy upon all men. Support me by thy Holy Spirit in the days of weakness and at the hour of death. And receive me at my death to everlasting happiness, for the sake of Jesus Christ. Amen."

This was the man who wrote:

> "Life is very short and uncertain. Let us spend it as well as we can."

And,

> "The principal use of prayer is to preserve in the mind a constant dependence on God."

Edmund Burke carried his coffin.

Chapter 2

Samuel Taylor Coleridge (1772–1834)

Coleridge was born at Ottery St Mary in Devon, the son of the local vicar. He was an outstanding scholar almost from the time of his infancy, and appointed Senior Grecian at Christ's Hospital, after which he studied for the priesthood of the Church of England at Jesus College, Cambridge. Imaginative, romantic and impetuous to an extent which often threatened his mental and physical health, he ran away from Cambridge and enlisted in the 15th Dragoons, a profession for which he was entirely ill-suited, and was rescued by efforts from his family.

The next implausible and fantastical enterprise to capture his interest came through his friendship with Robert Southey, who was then at Balliol. The year was 1794 and Europe was convulsed by revolutions. Coleridge and Southey were intoxicated by idealistic bliss and planned to form what they called a *pantisocracy* – a form of communist community – by the Susquehanna river in Pennsylvania. Of course, the idea was even more fanciful than his short-lived yen for soldiering and it came to nothing. In 1795 he married Sarah Fricker, a friend of Southey's.

Coleridge's first published writings were a few poems in the *Morning Chronicle* in 1793. By 1795 he was making a sparse living by lecturing and journalism in Bristol where he was also regarded for his eloquence as a preacher at various Unitarian chapels. He was befriended in Bristol by the bookseller Joseph Cottle who published his first collection of verse, *Poems on Various Subjects.* In 1797 he and Sarah moved to a cottage in Nether Stowey, Somerset where they met William and Dorothy Wordsworth.

In their collaboration on *Lyrical Ballads*, Wordsworth and

Coleridge together produced nothing short of a revolution in English poetry, rejecting the neo-classical and Augustan forms which by that time had degenerated into artificiality. This volume contained many startlingly original poems opening with Coleridge's *Rime of the Ancient Mariner* and ending with Wordsworth's *Tintern Abbey*. In 1798–99 he visited Germany with the Wordsworths and fell under the influence of German idealism, especially Kant. He also translated Schiller's *Piccolomini*.

In 1800 the Coleridges settled at Keswick in the Lake District and also spent time with the Wordsworths at Grasmere. Unfortunately he became addicted to opium. As a consequence he was dissolute, dejected and tortured by guilt. In this condition he wrote *Ode to Dejection* which was largely a confession of moral failure. Another result of Coleridge's deterioration was the increasing strain in his relationship with Wordsworth. Really, Wordsworth despaired of him and they finally ended their friendship in 1810 and moved to London.

Coleridge began *The Friend*, a weekly paper which ran for twenty-eight issues and was published as a book in 1818. He continued to write sporadically and lectured, chiefly on Shakespeare, at the Royal Institution. His play *Remorse* was a minor triumph at Drury Lane and he also published *Christabel* and the unfinished *Kubla Khan*.

He never recovered his hope of regaining his creative, inspirational powers but the wonder is that, in spite of his chronic ill-health and dejection, he published what has for almost two centuries been regarded as the finest literary criticism in English *Biographia Literaria* (1817). His *Aids to Reflection* (1825) contains his best theological and metaphysical work and his deepest spiritual and pastoral insights.

T.S. Eliot said of him:

"Coleridge was one of those persons – Donne, I suspect, was such another – of whom one might say, that if they had not been poets, they might have made something of their lives, might even have had a career; or conversely, that if they had not been interested in so many things, they might have been great poets."

Eliot's words were not intended as disparagement. On the contrary, they show clear insight into the character of Coleridge's tragic genius.

There has always been a widespread impression of Samuel Taylor Coleridge as a wayward, erratic genius, inspired yet muddled; someone who talked and talked without ever coming to any clear conclusion. He once said to his friend Charles Lamb,

"I believe that you have heard me preach?"

And Lamb replied,

"Why, I never heard you do anything else!"

Byron, too, poked fun at him in *Don Juan*:

"And Coleridge too has lately taken wing,
But like a hawk encumbered with his hood –
Explaining metaphysics to the nation –
I wish he would explain his Explanation".

Coleridge himself complained about this treatment, saying that he was constantly misunderstood and misinterpreted:

"Whatever therefore appeared with my name was condemned beforehand as predestined metaphysics."

These criticisms are unjust. Coleridge is not muddled, but he is difficult. And he is difficult because his thought is not consecutive, which does not mean that his thought is illogical – only that it is many-layered, as he sees so many aspects of a problem at once. He is, as it were, forever interrupting himself to explain the new thought which has just leapt into his head. He seems to see ideas as if they were in front of him as physical objects in space. He was pre-eminently what I have described as an embodied, incarnate thinker and extraordinarily acute. In this he can be compared in modern times with the philosopher Wittgenstein, who was similarly difficult and allusive but who was also stamped with the same mark of indubitability.

Coleridge's thought begins with a remarkably well-developed capacity for making crucial distinctions. The difference he draws between *imagination* and *fancy* is well-known; but here he is on *opposites* and *contraries*:

> "Permit me to draw your attention to the essential difference between *opposite* and *contrary*. Opposite powers are always of the same kind and tend to union. Thus the plus and minus poles of the magnet, positive and negative electricity, are opposites. Sweet and sour are opposites; sweet and bitter are contraries. The feminine character is *opposed* to the masculine; but the effeminate is its *contrary*."

And here, for example, is a typically Wittgensteinian distinction – but it happens to be Coleridge's:

> "To *think* of a thing is different from to *perceive* it as *to walk* is from *to feel the ground under you*."

Again, Wittgenstein says in *Tractatus Logico Philosophicus*:

> "It is not *how* the world is that is mystical, but *that* the world is."

But more than a century before Wittgenstein, Coleridge wrote in the *Notebooks*:

> "Good heaven! That there should be anything at all – and not nothing!"

Coleridge's thought, his whole outlook, should be understood as devotional or religious. He related to ideas as if they were living souls and so, where others would grow lonely if left to their own thoughts for too long, he lived among ideas as among a crowd of friends. So voluminous was he that it is difficult to know where to start when trying to get to grips with him. Perhaps as good a place as any would be to distinguish between his social religion and his personal religion. Turning first to the social aspect, thoroughly defined and discussed in his *On the Constitution of the Church and State,* we see that he says the purpose of the Church of England is to make civilisation *cultivated:*

> "Civilisation is itself but a mixed good, if not far more a corrupting influence, the hectic of disease, not the bloom of health, a nation so distinguished to be called a varnished than a polished people; where this civilisation is not grounded in *cultivation*, in the harmonious development of those qualities and faculties that characterise our *humanity*. We must be men in order to be citizens."

The purpose of life, that is its final cause, what Coleridge calls its *idea*, is that men should,

> "...be led by the supernatural in themselves."

He defines this idea as follows:

> "By an *idea* I mean that conception of a thing which is not abstracted from any particular state, form or mode in which the thing may happen to exist at this or that time; nor yet generalised from any number or succession of such forms or modes; but which is given by the knowledge of *its ultimate aim*."

Thus his thought is profoundly teleological: the world, including the world of ideas, has a destination. And although we notice Coleridge speaking of the need for *cultivation,* as part of the ultimate purpose or *idea* of a man, he is not

45

Matthew Arnold, no mere proponent of *sweetness and light*, and he is fiercely against the utilitarian calculus of Bentham. The aim, purpose and destination of which he speaks is beyond all utilitarian concerns: it is a divinely given vocation in which humankind partakes of God's supernatural nature and comes to realise the being of God as immanent within each soul and personality. To regard oneself lower than this would be to become less than human. So Coleridge warns us against using others merely as means to our own ends:

"One of the heart-depraving temptations of men in power as governors etc is to make *instruments* of their fellow creatures. The moment they find a man of honour or talent, instead of loving and esteeming him, they wish to *use* him. Hence that self-betraying side and down look of cunning.

"For it is impossible to conceive a *man* without the idea of God, eternity, freedom, will, absolute truth, of the good, the true, the beautiful, the infinite. An *animal* endowed with a memory of appearances and facts might remain. But the *man* will have vanished, and you have instead a creature more subtle than any beast of the field, but likewise cursed above every beast of the field; upon the belly it must go and dust must it eat all the days of this life. But I recall myself from a train of thought little likely to find favour in this age of sense and selfishness."

This cultivation which we should seek, the very *idea* for which we were created, is not realised by the individual alone; rather it is mediated through,

"...the true historical feeling, the mortal life of an historical nation, generation linked to generation by faith, freedom, heraldry and ancestral fame."

Alas, he sees that this high vocation has given place to,

"... the superstitions of wealth and newspaper reputation...talents without genius; a swarm of clever, well-informed men; an anarchy of minds, a despotism of maxims; despotism of finance in government and legislation; guess-work of general consequences substituted for moral and political philosophy..."

Once we cease from regarding God as both the goal of our existence and the indwelling means by which we attain this goal, we do not forfeit the divine spark in us, but we lose our humanity – because that humanity is created by God and meant to enjoy life with him in this world here and now. Rather than this *anarchy of minds and guesswork of general consequences* we require, in order to be guided in this living companionship with God,

"...a permanent, nationalised learned order, a national clerisy or church as an essential element of a rightly-constituted nation, without which it wants alike for its permanence and progression; and for which neither tract societies not conventicles, nor Lancastrian schools, nor mechanics' institutions, nor lecture bazaars under the absurd name of universities, nor all those collectively can be a substitute. For they are all marked with the same asterisk of spuriousness, show the same distemper-spot on the front, that they are empirical specifics for morbid *symptoms* that help to feed and continue the disease."

Although Coleridge envisioned this national clerisy as comprising other learned men apart from parsons, he yet saw a clear function for the clergy:

"To every parish throughout the kingdom there is transplanted a germ of civilisation; that in the remotest villages there is a nucleus, around which the capabilities of the place may crystallise and brighten; a model sufficiently superior to excite; yet sufficiently near to encourage and facilitate imitation."

Coleridge had read thoroughly the Anglican divines of the 16th and 17th centuries, especially Hooker and Law, and his model of a parson was a man such as George Herbert:

> "The clergyman is with his parishioners and among them; he is neither in the cloistered cell, nor in the wilderness, but a neighbour and a family man whose education and rank admit him to the mansion of the rich landholder, while his duties make him a frequent visitor of the farm-house and the cottage."

Again Coleridge makes a crucial distinction between what he calls *permanence* – the land – and what is *progressive* – the arts and sciences and the mercantile interests. Both permanence and progression are required in a healthy nation. But, as C.H. Sisson pointed out,

> "Coleridge's distinction goes to the root of the matter. Any political unity worth maintaining, or which is anyway to be maintained at all, must contain a principle of foresight and continuity which goes beyond the next set of trade figures; and it will be the foresight of care rather than calculation."

This realisation of the need for permanence is one of the insights which makes Coleridge's thought so pertinent to our present arrangements in which short-termism and the quick fix are often all there is to public policy-making.

It is the parson who has a foot in what is permanent and in what is progressive from which he derives his foresight of care. As Sisson remarks,

> "Where Bagehot sees the legitimate pursuits of men entitled to their complacency, Coleridge sees, *the drunken stupor of usurious selfishness; but men ought to be weighed, not counted.*"

For Coleridge, the clergyman is the instrument of both

permanence and progression. He loosens up, as it were, the permanence and anchors what is progressive in what abides:

> "The revenues of the church are in some sort of reversionary property of every family that may have a member educated for the church, or a daughter that may marry a clergyman. Instead of being foreclosed or immoveable, it is in fact the only species of landed property that is essentially moving and circulated."

Coleridge was radical in his support for the Catholic Emancipation Act of 1829, but he would not allow Roman Catholic priests to be members of the clerisy:

> "There are only two absolute disqualifications, and these are: allegiance to a foreign power or the acknowledgement of any other visible Head of the Church but our Sovereign Lord the King; and compulsory celibacy in connection with, and in dependence on, a foreign and extra-national Head."

So speaks an English patriot and true disciple of the Reformation, of which he adds,

> "Christianity itself was at stake; the cause was that of Christ in conflict with Antichrist."

Despite these vehement words, Coleridge denies the charge of anti-Catholicism:

> "It is not the Catholic Church as such that I attack, but Popery, built as it is on lies, implanted by the most abominable of despotisms, contrary to Christ's law and his inalienable mandate, and jeopardising the peace and security of every Church and State."

That is to say, Coleridge opposes the identification of the

Christian Church with any temporal power:

> "The Christian Church, I say, is no state, kingdom or realm of this world; nor is it an estate of any such realm, kingdom or state; but it is the appointed opposite to them all *collectively* – the *sustaining, correcting, befriending* Opposite of the world."

The Christian Church, he says, is,

> "The great redemptive process which began in the separation of light from Chaos (Hades or the Indistinction) and has its end in the union of life with God."

One might ask how, since he distinguishes the Christian Church from any temporal realm, he can wax so enthusiastic for the Sovereign as the Head of the Church of England. He answers,

> "Because there exists, God be thanked, a Catholic and Apostolic Church *in* England: and I thank God also for the constitutional and ancestral Church *of* England."

The temporal church of which the Sovereign is Head, may serve the eternal church of which Christ is the Head; but the two must be distinguished. So, as John Barrell comments,

> "Coleridge was anxious to support the granting of Catholic Relief, but only if it were accompanied by securities to protect the institutions which are the subject of his book *Church and State* from any attempt by Rome to establish a political base in England."

He vigorously opposed the idea that the Roman Catholic Church should ever be recognised as an Estate of the Realm: by this he meant that the Roman Catholic Clergy should not enjoy any part of the national wealth set apart for the National Church.

Well, it might be said that 19th century England is a faraway country of which we know little; but the profound issues raised in *On the Constitution of the Church and State* reverberate still. Sisson says,

"This is a remarkable book and certainly one which every literate Englishman should read. The *blessed accident* – which is how Coleridge saw Christianity or the Church of Christ in relation to the National Church – has ceased to exist in that relationship. It has no intelligibility. What then is the position of the theological rump in our now lay, secularised clerisy? There are three possibilities. They can stay and fight their corner, struggling for an intelligibility which might come again, and will come, if it is the truth they are concerned with. They can sit on pillars in some recess of the national structure, waiting for better times. Or they can let their taste for having an ecclesiastical club carry them into one or other of those international gangs of opinion – that which has its headquarters in Rome or that which has a shadowy international meeting-place in Canterbury. In any case it will be a *political* choice that is being made. For my part, I shall prefer those who stay and fight their corner, content to be merely the Church in a place."

Church and State was published in 1830. Reading it again in 2014, as civilisation is confronted by worldwide jihadism, the mind is startled by what might seem to be a final example of extraordinary prescience:

"That erection of a temporal monarch under the pretence of a spiritual authority, which was not possible in Christendom but by the extinction or entrancement of the spirit of Christianity, and which has therefore been only partially attained by the Papacy – this was effected in full by Mahomet, to the establishment of the most extensive and complete despotism that ever warred against civilisation and the interests of humanity."

Opium was not Coleridge's only addiction. He was a compulsive writer and his personal religious thoughts are found in everything he wrote, particularly in his hundreds of notebooks where the most sublime insights are wedged on the page next to a weather report. As Seamus Perry says in his *Introduction* to the notebooks,

> "Here his response to Kantian philosophy stands next to exquisite accounts of the sun setting in Borrowdale. For Coleridge, our most abstract poet-metaphysician, is also one of our greatest laureates of *things*."

Coleridge's views on personal religion appear most systematically in *Biographia Literaria* and *Aids to Reflection*. And the most acute and perceptive among all his insights were derived from Kant during the visit he made with the Wordsworths to Germany. It is a remarkable man indeed who sets out to teach himself the German language by reading *The Critique of Pure Reason*, but that is what Coleridge did, and Kant remained the dominant intellectual influence on him for the rest of his life. He was overwhelmed by Kant's demonstration of the necessity of transcendence.

Bryan Magee sums up Kant's long, meandering transcendental argument as follows:

> "No philosophy that equates reality with actual or possible experience can be right. Because all the ways in which we can apprehend material objects, whether sensorily or mentally, are directly or indirectly experience-dependent, and therefore subject-dependent, such objects cannot exist independently of us and of our experience *in any of the ways in which we apprehend them*."

In other words, the way things appear in the empirical world, and according to science, cannot be the way things really are in themselves. Magee adds,

> "The notion of objectivity is of incalculable value in

science, and yet it is a metaphysical construct of our minds."

It follows that,

"...the self is not a possible object of observation or experience, and therefore not a possible object of empirical knowledge."

And,

"Human beings do not consist solely of our bodies; in addition to having bodies, we have or are selves, and these selves are not empirical objects in the natural world; also that morals and values do not have their existence solely within the natural world."

Most philosophers who try to deduce the freedom of the will, deduce or infer this freedom from, say, the fact of the existence of God – or some other benign set of governing circumstances. Kant does the opposite: he says, in effect, that because we *know already* that our wills are free, we can claim direct knowledge of the moral law which is the will of God. In 1798 when Coleridge visited Germany, it was but seventeen years after the publication of the *Critique of Pure Reason*. Coleridge was certainly one of the first English scholars to read that volume of which it has been said, it marked a Copernican revolution in philosophy. Coleridge was captivated:

"The writings of the illustrious seer of Konigsberg, the founder of the critical philosophy, more than any other work at once invigorated and disciplined my understanding. The originality, the depth and the compression of his thoughts; the novelty and subtlety, yet solidity and importance of the distinctions; the adamantine chain of the logic; and I will venture to add – paradox as it will appear to those who have taken their notion of Immanuel

Kant from reviewers and Frenchmen – the clearness and evidence of the *Critique of Pure Reason*; of the metaphysical elements of natural philosophy; and of his religion within the bounds of pure reason, took possession of me as with the giant's hand."

Coleridge became a Kantian in his opinions as to religious belief and yet, being Coleridge, he shaped his Kantianism according to his own idiosyncratic mould. He wrote in 1825,

"What we cannot imagine, we cannot in the proper sense conceive. Whatever is representable in the forms of time and space is nature. But whatever is included in time and space is included in the mechanism of cause and effect. And conversely, whatever has its principle in itself, so far as to originate its actions" – a clear reference to the will – "cannot be contemplated in any of the forms of space and time. It must therefore be considered as spirit or spiritual."

Rosemary Ashton comments:

"Coleridge's study of Kant in particular, bears fruit in his characterisation of the previous age, the 18th century, as materialist, mechanist, empirical; while the present age, the 19th century, by contrast, is, or ought to be spiritual."

In *Aids to Reflection*, Coleridge's whole tilt was against that materialist, mechanistic, empirical prejudice – what he called *the mechanico-corpuscular philosophy* – and against William Paley's *Evidences (1794)* in particular. He railed against associationism, empiricism and mechanism when, as in Paley's writings, those methods were used to justify religion:

"How plausible and popular this is to the great majority! They will accept the doctrine for their make-faith. And why? Because it is feeble. And whatever is feeble is always plausible: for it favours mental indolence."

Against Paley, he wrote,

> "Evidences? I am weary of evidences. Only rouse a man and make him *feel* the truth of his religion."

But this was no mere subordination of evidence or argument to feelings – and especially not to aesthetic feelings of the kind which George Santayana referred to as *emotional shocks*. Rather Coleridge is much closer to Pascal's understanding of feelings and *heart* where Pascal says, *The heart has its reasons which reason does not know. We feel it in a thousand things.*

Since we know, through the access which our freewill gives us to the moral law, that we are not the authors of our own being, we also know that our minds are, or can become, copies of the mind of God. Coleridge explains how:

> "The primary imagination I hold to be the living power and prime agent of all human perception, and as a repetition in the finite mind of the eternal act of creation in the infinite I AM."

If one might so put it, the mind is a copy of the mind of the Creator; therefore true doctrine reveals our true nature and our nature's relationship with God. In order to achieve knowledge of God and the awareness of God's presence, we need first imagination and then reflective reason:

> "The interest aimed at was to consist in the interesting of the affections by the dramatic truth of such emotions as would naturally accompany such situations *supposing them real.*"

In describing the occasion of the *Lyrical Ballads*, Coleridge famously says,

> "We transfer from our inward nature a human interest and a semblance of truth sufficient to procure for these

shadows of imagination that willing suspension of disbelief for the moment which constitutes poetic faith."

In seeking true understanding, one should not look at the world with the empirical eye:

"In looking at objects of nature, while I am thinking. As at yonder moon dim-glimmering through the dewy window-pane, I seem rather to be seeking, as it were *asking*, a symbolical language for something within me that already and forever exists, than observing anything new. Even when that latter is the case, yet still I have always an obscure feeling as if that new phenomenon were the dim awaking of a forgotten or hidden truth of my inner nature. It is still interesting as Word, a symbol. It is *Logos* – the Creator and the Evolver."

That sensational judgement looks backwards to Plato and the Gospel of St John and forwards to T.S. Eliot and his *objective correlative.*

This method in poetry is the same method Coleridge takes with him in his attempts at religious understanding.

He urges us to reasoned reflection and instructs us how to begin:

"Dwell at home. It is surprising that the greater part of mankind cannot be prevailed upon at least to visit themselves sometimes. An hour of solitude passed in sincere and earnest prayer, or the conflict with and conquest over a single passion or a subtle bosom sin, will teach more of thought, will more effectively awaken the faculty and form the habit of reflection than a year's study in the schools without them."

This saying reminds us of Pascal's complaint that all the troubles of the world arise out of a man's inability sit quietly in his own room for half an hour. In our times, beguiled as we are by electronic gadgetry and the banal diversions of cyberspace, it is hard to believe that we have made much improvement on the way things were in Coleridge's day. What is it that keeps us perennially from real and wholesome reflection which can do us so much good? Coleridge answers:

> "The most frequent impediment to men's turning their minds inward upon themselves is that they are afraid of what they shall find there. There is an aching hollowness in the bosom, a dark, cold speck at the heart."

But we should take courage and try regularly,

> "...to form the human mind anew after the divine image."

Reasonable reflection makes us understand that Christian truth is the satisfaction that we only intermittently but desperately crave:

> "The sense, the inward feeling in the soul of each believer of its exceeding *desirableness* – the experience that he *needs* something, joined with the strong foretokening that the redemption and the graces propounded to us in Christ are *what* he needs – this I hold to be the true foundation of the spiritual edifice."

He says,

> "Christianity is not a theory or a speculation, but a life – not a philosophy of life, but a life and a living process. Try it."

How? Coleridge spells it out for us:

> "It is the experience derived from a practical conformity to the conditions of the gospel – it is the opening eye; the dawning light; the terrors and the promises of spiritual growth; the blessedness of loving God as God;

the nascent sense of sin, hatred of sin, and of the incapability of attaining to either without Christ; it is the sorrow that still rises up from beneath, and the consolation that meets it from above."

All these things are discovered indubitably by reasonable reflection. In short,

"Reason and religion are their own evidence."

I began by comparing Coleridge with Wittgenstein, and we discover that Wittgenstein held remarkably similar views on the nature of religion. In his jottings, collected in *Culture and Value*, Wittgenstein says:

"Christianity is not a doctrine, not, I mean, a theory about what has happened and will happen to the human soul, but a description of something that actually takes place in human life. For 'consciousness of sin' is a real event and so are despair and salvation through faith. Those who speak of such things (Bunyan, for instance) are simply describing what has happened to them, whatever gloss anyone may want to put on it."

As Wittgenstein continues, we feel it could be Coleridge talking:

"The way to solve the problem you see in life is to live in a way that will make what is problematic disappear. The fact that life is problematic shows that the shape of your life does not fit into life's mould. So you must change the way you live and, once your life does fit into the mould, what is problematic will disappear. Don't we have the feeling that someone who sees no problem in life is blind to something important, even to the most important thing of all? Don't I feel like saying that a man like that is just living aimlessly – blindly, like a mole, and that if only he could see, he would see the problem? Or shouldn't I say rather: a man who lives rightly won't experience the problem as *sorrow*, so for him it will not be a problem, but a joy rather; in other words for him, it will be a bright halo round his life, not a dubious background."

Reflection brings with it the sense of our imperfection and our need to be saved from something. The enemy of salvation is the denial of the truth that there is a need for salvation. And today there are plenty of *progressive* people about to tell us that we have no such need – the Pelagians who deny Original Sin, who tell us we are fine as we are. Coleridge exposes the sentimentality which is at the root of our narcissistic self-esteeming:

"All the evil achieved by Hobbes and the whole school of materialists will appear inconsiderable if it be compared with the mischief effected and occasioned by the sentimental philosophy of Lawrence Sterne. The vilest appetites and the most remorseless inconstancy acquired the titles *of the heart...the irresistible feelings...the too tender sensibility.*"

The antidote to sentimentality is not disembodied intellectuality but the discovery deep within ourselves those feelings which are real. In the *Notebooks* he says:

"Real pain can alone cure us of imaginary ills. We feel a thousand miseries till we are lucky enough to feel Misery."

It is precisely the feelings which need to be educated, and they become educated by the Divine reason:

"I do not wish you to act from truths. Still and always act from your feelings. But only meditate often on these truths, that some time or other they may become your feelings."

And he prays:

"O make reason spread light over our feelings to make our feelings diffuse vital warmth through our reason."

It is an insight which anticipates Kierkegaard.

Coleridge nowhere claims that religious faith is easily achieved. In fact, he counsels against easiness in believing:

"Never be afraid to doubt. He never truly believed who was not made first sensible and convinced of unbelief."

But he adds the caution,

"Everyone is to give a reason for his faith."

And, as we have seen, for Coleridge reason is never an abstract explanation, but the means by which we come to see that the human need and the divine supply are always conjoined: the second is the answer to what the first is the question. There is, I think, among all the misinterpretations of Coleridge, one that surpasses them all. It concerns his famous saying,

"He who begins by loving Christianity more than truth, will proceed to love his own sect or church more than Christianity, and end by loving himself more than all."

This is often taken to mean that there is some objective standard of truth by which Christianity can be judged true or false, as it were, *academically*. But this thought is far from Coleridge's mind: what he urges the reader to do, by reflection, reason and imaginative meditation, is to persevere until he sees that Christianity and truth are the same thing. And this same thing is not *theoretical*: it is the deepest we can achieve.

It is not achieved overnight. Coleridge urges us to go easy on ourselves, not to expect too much too soon. He says,

"Translate the theological terms into their moral equivalents, saying, *This may not be all that is meant, but this is meant, and it is that portion of the meaning which belongs to me in this present state of my progress. For example, render the words, 'sanctification of the Spirit' by' purity in life and action from a pure principle'."*

As always, here again is the retreat from abstractions into what is tangible, embodied. Coleridge does not regularly achieve this embodiment in his poetry, with the exception of *The Ancient Mariner* and a few other fragments. But the prose of his literary criticism and that found in his spiritual reflections shows that he was a great poet particularly when he was not explicitly writing poetry! Here, for instance, is an extract from something he wrote in his *Notebooks* about his voyage to Malta in 1830:

> "Thought of a lullaby song, to a child on a ship: great rocking cradle...creak of main top irons, rattle of ropes and squeak of the rudder...and so play Bo-peep with the rising moon and the lizard light. There is thy native country, boy! Whither art thou going to?"

The packed images in that breathtaking short piece look forward to Pound's first *Canto*:

> "And then went down to the ship,
> Set keel to breakers, forth on the godly sea, and
> We set up mast and sail on that swart ship..."

How to define such consciousness? Coleridge's answer is direct and surprising:

> "Conscience is the ground and antecedent of consciousness"

And it is reasonable reflection which awakes our conscience and stimulates us into spiritual awareness. We must not expect ourselves to be better than we are. As we are commanded to have mercy on our neighbour, so we should deal mercifully with ourselves:

> "Art thou under the tyranny of sin – a slave to vicious habits – at enmity with God, and a skulking fugitive from thine own conscience? The best and most Christian-like pity thou canst show is to take pity on thine own soul. The best and most acceptable service thou canst render is to do justice and show mercy to thyself."

For love is indivisible. And as he says,

> "Love transforms the soul into a conformity with the object loved."

Which is why we must be careful in choosing the things to love.

All these deepest things can be apprehended by reason. As Claude Welch said of Coleridge's high understanding of reason and faith,

> "Faith must be a reasoning faith, but reason must be understood more deeply than either by rationalism or the religion of the heart. There *are* mysteries in Christianity, but these are reason in its highest form of self-affirmation."

What are mysteries to us are part of the Divine reason.

Welch briefly and brilliantly encapsulates what religion meant to Coleridge:

> "His own sense of the quality and character of personal religion is one in which prayer and the struggle of sin and redemption were at the centre. For Coleridge, in contrast to Hegel, *Let us pray* represented a higher form of activity than, *Let us think about God.*"

Finally in Coleridge the poet is at one with the theologian as revealed in a magnificent passage such as this from *Aids to Reflection*:

"Linger not in the justice court, listening to thy indictment. Loiter not in waiting to hear the sentence. No, anticipate the verdict. Appeal to Caesar. Haste to the King for a pardon. Struggle thitherward, though in fetters; and cry aloud and collect the whole remaining strength of thy will in thy outcry, 'Lord, I believe. Help thou mine unbelief!' Disclaim all right of property in thy fetters. Say that they belong to the old man, and that thou dost but carry them to the grave to be buried with their owner! Fix thy thought on what Christ did, what Christ *is* – as if thou wouldst fill the hollowness of thy soul with Christ. If he emptied himself of glory to become sin for thy salvation, must not thou be emptied of thy sinful self to become righteousness in and through his agony and the effective merits of his Cross?"

And there is this from the conclusion of *Biographia Literaria:*

"I have earnestly endeavoured to kindle young minds, and to guard them against the temptations of scorners, by showing that the scheme of Christianity as taught in the liturgy and homilies of our church, though not discoverable by human reason, is yet in accordance with it: that link follows link by necessary consequence; that religion passes out of the ken of reason only where the eye of reason has reached its own horizon; and that faith is then but its continuation: even as the day softens away into the sweet twilight, and twilight, hushed and breathless, steals into the darkness. It is night, sacred night..."

This is beginning to sound like Bruckner!

"...where the upraised eye views only the starry heaven which manifests itself alone: and the outward beholding is fixed on the sparks twinkling in the awful depth, though suns of other worlds, only to preserve the soul steady and collected in its pure act of inward adoration to the great I AM, and to the filial WORD that re-affirmeth it from eternity to eternity, whose choral echo is the universe."

Samuel Taylor Coleridge, as Charles Lamb affectionately recalled him,

"An archangel, a little damaged."

Chapter Three

John Henry Newman (1801–1890)

Newman was born in London, the son of a City banker and his mother was a deeply spiritual Calvinist of the moderate, Arminian variety. Newman's upbringing was greatly influenced by his mother's piety and he writes movingly at the beginning of *Apologia Pro Vita Sua* of his early heartfelt Evangelicalism. He went up to Trinity College, Oxford aged sixteen, took a second class degree and was elected a fellow of Oriel where he met those other High Churchmen, Pusey and Froude.

In 1824 he was ordained in the Church of England and attained the living of St Mary's, Oxford in 1828. In 1832–33 Newman went with Froude and Froude's father on a Mediterranean tour and it was during this period that he wrote many of his early poems which later appeared in his *Lyra Apostolica*, also the renowned hymn *Lead Kindly Light.*

When parliament suppressed ten Irish bishoprics in 1833, and John Keble preached his Oxford assize sermon on National Apostasy, Newman was in the congregation. This occasion marked the beginning of the Tractarian, or Oxford, Movement to which Newman contributed a number of tracts, including the most controversial Tract Ninety (1841) in which he argued that *The Thirty-nine Articles* were Catholic in spirit. This argument was widely judged implausible and it was then that many of the Tractarians realised that their aim to find in the Church of England a *via media* between Rome and Protestantism was impossible and became Roman Catholics. Newman agonised for two more years before resigning his parish in 1843 and retiring to nearby Littlemore. In October 1845 he was received into the Roman Catholic Church.

After studying in Rome for a year, he was ordained priest, returning to England to establish a branch of the Oratarians at Edgbaston, Birmingham. Here he did much pastoral work among the poor during the cholera epidemic of 1849.

His lectures *Anglican Difficulties* were published in 1850, followed by his *Catholicism in England* (1851) and *The Idea of a University* (1852) which he wrote while Rector of Dublin Catholic University, a post he held from 1851–58. Throughout the 1840s and 1850s he preached numerous brilliant sermons and these too received wide publication and public attention.

In 1864 began the great controversy which caused Newman to write his *Apologia*. The evangelical Charles Kingsley wrote an article in *Macmillan's Magazine* in which he said,

"Truth, for its own sake, had never been a virtue with the Roman clergy. Father Newman informs us that it need not, and on the whole ought not to be."

Newman's defence was in the form of one of the finest of all volumes of Christian apologetics.

In 1865 he published his magnificent long poem *The Dream of Gerontius*. His *Grammar of Assent* (1870) is a very finely discriminating work of philosophical theology, building on the place of analogy in talking about the faith and introducing new arguments in favour of belief, which he described as *convergent probability.*

Newman became much embroiled in ecclesiastical politics around the time of the Vatican Council. He opposed the extreme faction – the so called *Ultramontanes*, led by Cardinal Manning. For his support in these controversies, Pope Leo XIII invited Newman to Rome in 1879 and appointed him Cardinal. He returned to Edgbaston where he died in 1890.

In his novel *Decline and Fall*, Evelyn Waugh writes,

"There is a species of person called a Modern Churchman

who draws the full salary of a beneficed clergyman yet does not commit himself to any religious belief."

These types talk a great deal about God, but it is clear from everything they say that they do not really believe in him – except as some sort of metaphor for a certain sort of social and political activism. They have watered-down the Christian faith so that the Ten Commandments have become merely the ten suggestions. They invent the sorts of prayers adjusted to their new *Christianity-lite* and put them in a new prayer book. And what is the purpose of the newfangled book? As Dean Inge said,

"Revised Prayer Books? Only the attempt to suppress burglary by licensing petty larceny."

Newman saw the beginnings of this programme of reductionism as long ago as the 1830s and he opposed it vigorously. He was one of the first to see what the final effects of the so-called *liberals* – really unbelieving – clergymen would be. He said,

"The tendency of the age is towards liberalism. But truly, religion must be based on authority of some kind – not upon sentimentality. It is the church which is the only legitimate guarantor of religious truth. The liberals know this and are in every possible manner trying to break it up."

He foresaw the time when bishops and archbishops would undermine the authority of the Bible; our time in which leading theologians say that Scripture is a collection of fables which have to be *demythologised*; men – and increasingly women – for whom the miracles of Our Lord are regarded as very doubtful tales indeed. The 19th century saw the rise of the new historical-critical school of biblical interpretation in Germany which was ideologically based on the prejudices of scientific materialism: the assumption was, *If supernatural, then not historical.* The 20th century theologian Rudolf Bultmann was even more explicit and declared,

"You cannot believe in the miracle stories of the New Testament in an age of electric light and the wireless."

He did not pause to explain why not. Bultmann was lionised in the university departments of theology and among ordinands forty years ago. He was part of the supposed enlightenment of the 1960s when *liberation* was the word on everybody's lips, when traditional teaching was despised as something properly abandoned by *man come of age.* The trademark of liberal theology is reductionism and denial and the titles of some of the principal books and articles of this sort published over the last forty years give this away: *Our Image of God Must Go; But That I Can't Believe; The Myth of God Incarnate; The Secular Meaning of the Gospel; The Gospel of Christian Atheism; Objections to Christian Belief.* The book which made debunking truly fashionable was J.A.T. Robinson's *Honest to God* (1963) – its title contriving to suggest that all previous ages had been dishonest until honest John Robinson turned up to tell us the truth. And what was this truth? That God is no more *metaphysically out there* than he had previously been supposed to have been *literally and physically up there.* Though it would be hard to find any serious students of the Bible or of theology in general who were ever attracted by such crass literalism. Really the liberal theologians were attacking aunt Sallys.

Newman saw all this coming, including the relativising of the concept of *truth* to the point of its abolition, as by the post-modernist philosophers and the deconstructionist theories of such as Jacques Derrida and Michel Foucault. Naturally, the denial of absolute truths in theology was followed by the relativising of morality. Chapter six of *Honest to God* introduced us to *situation ethics* which located personal responsibility not in adherence to Commandments but in *doing the loving thing in the situation in which one finds oneself.* So, together with the new theology, there came the new morality – which one critic described as *only the old immorality in a miniskirt*

Newman concluded that the reason for the rise of liberal theology lay in the fact that the clergy had never been properly taught. He said,

> "There is a lack of interest in doctrine among the clergy who are so utterly ignorant of the subject thanks to their lack of any proper theological education. Instead of regarding the sacraments and the doctrines of the creed as the basics, liberals, imbued with the rationalistic assumptions of the Enlightenment, were busy constructing an abstract system of criticism which presumed to evaluate and find wanting these basic rites and teachings."

Of this process, Newman said:

> "To rationalise in matters of revelation is to make our reason the standard and measure of the doctrines revealed; to stipulate that those doctrines should be rejected if they come in collision with our existing opinions or habits of thought, or are with difficulty harmonised with our existing stock of knowledge. It is rationalism which accepts the revelation and then explains it away; to speak of it as the word of God but to treat it as the word of man; to refuse to let it speak for itself; to claim to be told the why and the how of God's dealings with us... to frame some gratuitous hypothesis about the doctrines of the faith and then to garble, gloss and colour them, to trim, clip, pare away and twist them in order to bring them into conformity with the idea to which we have subjected them. This is to illustrate how the age of railroads is bound to behave towards the age of martyrs."

He called this trend *doctrinal licentiousness*. It was beginning in his day but it is rampant in ours. Edward Norman spells it out for us in his book *Secularisation* where he says:

69

"Fewer and fewer expect to be instructed in doctrines or interpretations. Religion is becoming so individualised that *believers* expect to be able to make up their own understanding of Christianity, often by random selection from current ideals, some traditionally recognised within the church and some not...Where lay people are encouraged to work out religious ideas for themselves without reference to fixed doctrinal requirements, and where the clergy are principally trained with the intention that they shall assist them in this enterprise, and so all kinds of ideas enter the church. The Church of England has no effective means of resisting this process. Nor does it have the will to do so. It has become a willing partner in its internal secularisation; the first to re-evaluate its core message in terms of ordinary human welfare and emotional sustenance...Behold the fruits of theological liberalism: decades of reductionism and scepticism have so weakened the body that virtually anything can now enter it without serious challenge...For the Church of England something that is beginning to have the appearance of a meltdown is occurring...The leaders of the church do not appear to sense the present crisis as an ideological crisis at all. They are concerned about falling church attendance and about a whole range of organisational matters, but they appear unaware that the absence of a systematic teaching office is the root of all their difficulties."

This loss of all authority began in the 19th century when theologians and church leaders embraced the methods of the new historical-critical school and accepted the liberal teaching that the Bible and Christian tradition were to be understood in terms other than their own. We have reached the *meltdown* of which Edward Norman speaks because the liberal trend has been allowed to prevail for these last 150 years and to become ever more secularised and radicalised in the process. Moreover, our society is now so obsessed with pluralism and diversity and with post-modern epistemologies which deny any meaning to the word *truth*.

It is impossible for Christianity to survive in such a climate. For the time being, the appearances of the Christian faith conceal the fact that there is no underlying reality. The cathedrals and the churches are visible presences but, in all but a very few, what goes on within them has little to do with the historic and traditional faith. *The King James Bible* and *The Book of Common Prayer* have been sidelined and the Roman Church abandoned the Latin Mass in 1969 and effectually secularised its liturgy. The bishops retain their crooks, copes and mitres and the clergy their cassocks and surplices, but the historic faith to which these things bore witness is past its evanescence. Britain is a secular country. It is actually illegal to teach Christianity in our schools as *true*. Are we then to wonder that our children know nothing of the faith, even such a formative Christian utterance as the Lord's Prayer?

The process of secularisation has accelerated tremendously during the last twenty or thirty years. Until comparatively recently, we regarded ourselves as a Christian country. Our people thought of themselves, insofar as there was ever the need to consider such matters, as Christians. They were not devout. Churchgoing gradually declined from its peak in Victorian times and the rate of this decline increased after the First World War. The British people in the 20th century did not go in for family prayers before breakfast or for Bible reading after supper on Sunday. But, if you had asked them, they would have said they were Christian in the sense that they believed in *Do as you would be done by*. Unconsciously they had imbibed the biblical morality exemplified by the Ten Commandments from the Old Testament and the Sermon on the Mount from the New. They were unostentatious, non-pious people whose overriding sense of decency derived from the Judaeo-Christian tradition which had shaped the lives and the institutions of Britain for more than a thousand years.

As a boy, I spent some time in hospital and I remember the cards affixed to the bottom of each patient's bed identifying that person's religion – presumably in case of the swift onset of a critical emergency. Some of these were marked *RC* and there were one or two here and there which said *Jewish*. But the overwhelming proportion of them simply said *C. of E.* I never recall any indicating that the occupant of the bed was atheist or agnostic. And this was in the 1950s, before the coming of the multicultural society and so of course there were none marked *Hindu* or *Muslim.*

Sundays were special. There were such things as the Sunday Trading Laws and most of the shops were shut. There was no league football on Sundays.

Children were not allowed to play out in the street but were required to put on smarter clothes, *Sunday best.* It was a day altogether more sedate. Most families would end Sunday by taking an evening stroll into the park and listen to the brass band. Old men might be playing bowls there. But no one played cricket or kicked a ball around.

Other days were different too. All the shops and factories closed on Good Friday. There were no newspapers that day. Whitsunday was special. This Sunday, seven weeks after Easter, was in the north of England the day when children received their new clothes, their *Whitsuntide clothes*. And the tradition was that children – boys as well as girls – went round the suburb to visit grandparents, uncles and aunts who would admire your new outfit and give you sixpence. No one celebrated Halloween or Mothers' Day – still less the transatlantic novelty Fathers' Day. Christmas was kept joyfully but it started on Christmas Eve and not, as it seems these days, at the end of September. And Christmas ended the day after Boxing Day when everyone went back to work.

What makes Newman such an inspired prophet is that In the middle of the 19ᵗʰ century, he foresaw that all this would come to pass. He correctly indentified the root causes of secularisation and saw how it would proceed. He said,

"The Church's highest praise is only that it admits a variety of opinions...But why should God speak unless he meant to say something? If there has been a revelation, then there must be some essential doctrine proposed by it. To suppose that all beliefs are equally true in the eyes of God, provided they are all sincerely held, is simply unreal and a mere dream of reason. A system of doctrine has arisen in which faith or spiritual-mindedness is contemplated and rested on as the end of religion and not Christ. And in this way religion is made to consist in contemplating ourselves instead of Christ. Faith and spiritual-mindedness are dwelt on as ends and obstruct the view of Christ. Poor miserable captives to whom such doctrine is preached as the Gospel! What, is this the liberty wherewith Christ has made us free, and wherein we stand, the home of our own thoughts, the prison of our own sensations, the province of self? This is nothing but a specious idolatry."

All beliefs equally true so long as they are sincerely held... mere spiritual-mindedness...the church admits only a variety of opinions...the prison of our own sensations, the province of self...
This is where we are now in our sentimental, hedonistic, therapeutic, thoroughly diversified, relativised secular society. And Newman saw the rot setting in a century and a half ago. He wrote:

"The spirit at work against Christianity is latitudinarianism, indifference, republicanism and schism – a spirit which tries to overthrow doctrine as if it were the fruit of bigotry, and discipline as if the instrument of priest-craft. The prevailing lies of the age are that there is no positive truth in religion, and that any creed is as good as any other. The lie teaches that all religious declarations are equally worthy because they are no more than matters of personal opinion. The lie teaches that religion is not a truth but a sentiment or a taste; and it is the right of any individual to make of it whatever strikes his fancy."

Of course when religion becomes like that, there is no religion and this is our tragedy today. Tragedy, because the empty-headed debunking prejudice against traditional faith is cutting people off from what can really nourish them.

Newman saw that liberalism would lead eventually to amoralism and nihilism and he devoted his whole life and effort to providing the antidote. The antidote he provided is in the form of the Sacraments and the doctrines of the Creed. He spoke warmly of…

> "Bishop Butler's wonderfully gifted intellect which caught the idea that had actually been the rule in the primitive church of teaching the more Sacred Truths ordinarily by rites and ceremonies which persuade by their tenderness and mysteriousness."

Christian doctrines are true, he insisted. And their truth is the only reason for believing them. If the church thinks it can get by without believing the truth of its doctrines, then the church has in fact resigned.

Newman expressed in an exact paragraph what he calls *the Principle of Liberalism*:

> "That truth and falsehood in religion are but matters of opinion; that one doctrine is as good as another; that the Governor of the world does not intend that we should gain the truth; that there is no truth; that we are not more acceptable to God by believing this man than by believing that one; that no one is answerable for his opinions; that they are a matter of necessity or accident; that it is enough if we sincerely hold what we profess; that our merit lies in seeking, not in possessing; that it is a duty to follow what seems to us true; that it may be a gain to succeed, but can be no harm to fail; that we may take up and lay down opinions at pleasure; that we may safely trust to ourselves in matters of Faith and need no other guide."

The Post-Enlightenment liberals, who were the Establishment in Newman's age, believed that reason is immaculate: our feelings may turn us to the bad, but reason is an infallible guide if only we learn to follow its dictates accurately. But Newman reminds us:

"Reason is God's gift; but so are the passions: reason is as guilty as passion."

Moreover, reason does not operate in a vacuum. It is a process which follows from axioms and assumptions. People forget that axioms and assumptions are often little better than prejudices. Reason has to start from somewhere. For a thousand years and more the place from which western societies started was the Christian doctrine of man, of creation, fall, redemption and restoration.

Newman's words about *the expectation of success but without the corresponding fear of possible failure,* obviously common among the *bien pensants* of his day, is one of the main features of the political-correctness of our own day – and particularly in the area of education. In dealing with pupils, teachers are told to use *positive reinforcement* – as the Behaviourist Professor B.F.Skinner did with his rats and pigeons. This means emphasising rewards and adjuring punishments; but where there is no chance of blame, there can logically be no sense in the concept of praise. Virtue exists only in the face of vice.

Edward Norman wrote,

"The liberals are in possession of the places of learning and education and the media."

Newman regarded authentic teaching within a genuine university as essential for the continued understanding of the Christian Faith. In his *The Idea of a University* he said,

"A university is a place of teaching universal knowledge. It cannot fulfil its object duly without the church's assistance; or, to use the theological term, the church is necessary for its *integrity.* A university by its name professes to teach universal knowledge: theology is surely a branch of knowledge: how then is it possible to profess all branches of knowledge, and yet to exclude not the meanest or the narrowest of the number?"

Of course, some argued in Newman's time, as many more argue today, that theology is not a form of knowledge but only a matter of opinion. As we learnt from Newman, it is liberalism itself which has created this view. But Newman stoutly defends university theology:

"Are we to limit our idea of university knowledge by the evidence of our senses? Then we exclude history. By testimony? Then we exclude metaphysics. By abstract reasoning? Then we exclude physics. Is not the being of a God reported to us by testimony, handed down by history, inferred by an inductive process, brought home to us by metaphysical necessity, urged on us by the suggestions of our conscience?"

Moreover,

"In a state of society such as ours in which authority, prescription, tradition, habit, moral instinct and the divine influence go for nothing, in which patience of thought and depth and consistency of view are scorned as subtle and scholastic, in which free discussion and fallible judge-ment are prized as the birthright of each individual...all this I own it gentlemen frightens me."

He was right to be frightened – as we are who inhabit the age in which this nightmare – vision has come to be our daily reality.

But it is sometimes argued that pluralism and diversity of views are signs of a society's health. This point was asked of Newman himself:

"A question was put to me by a philosopher of the day: *Why cannot you go your way and let us go ours*? I answer in the name of theology, *When Newton can dispense with the metaphysician, then you may dispense with us.*"

In other words knowledge requires coherence and even,

especially, scientific knowledge requires absolute presuppositions – such as, that the world of nature is regular – and these absolute presuppositions are metaphysical. More than that, as we shall explore in greater detail in the chapter on R.G. Collingwood, the particular metaphysics required for the successful practice of modern science was that by which the Christian Fathers corrected the error in classical thought – the error that was responsible for the downfall of classical society. Newman understood this exactly:

"Does theology cast no light upon history? Has it no influence on the principles of ethics? Is it without any sort of bearing on physics, metaphysics and political science? Can we drop it out of the circle of knowledge without allowing either that that circle is thereby mutilated or on the other hand that theology is no science? In a word, religious truth is not only a portion but a condition of general knowledge. Religious doctrine is knowledge in as full a sense as Newton's doctrine is knowledge. University education without theology is simply un-philosophical. Theology has at least as good a right to claim a place there as astronomy."

Newman also recognised that moral philosophy and social policy require theological understanding and underpinning:

"It is not enough simply to see the evil and injustice and suffering of this world and precipitate oneself into action. We must know, what only theology can tell us, *why* these things are wrong. Otherwise we may right some wrongs at the cost of creating new ones. If this is a world in which I, and the majority of my fellow beings live in that perpetual distraction from God which exposes us to the one great peril, that of final and complete alienation from God after death, there is some wrong which I must try to help to put right."

C.S. Lewis's insight that *The abolition of God necessarily leads to the abolition of man.* derives directly from the writing of Newman.

In the public policy of his day, Newman saw through a political movement which went under the guise of liberalism while constantly acquiring for itself more centralisation and more authority. He said,

> "It is a growing peculiarity of the present age to purchase a respite from present actual evils by the introduction of it into various departments of the body politic to which it was before a stranger. It is now becoming the fashion to merge the nation with the government, whereas in the past private enterprise had led the way. Waterloo Bridge was built not by the government but by individuals."

To merge the nation with the government! This is exactly what has happened today with the deliberate destruction of the authority of parliament by the ruling political elite. And, like us, Newman too heard a great deal of chatter about *reforms* in his day and he saw their true purpose:

> "Recent reforms are all evidence of the growing popularity of the centralising system. But the destruction of local influences which centralisation involves and the disorganisation of parliament as the seat and instrument of administration tend to increase the power of the executive as the main-spring of all national power and virtually identical with the government."

For *reforms* read *corruptions.* And he bemoaned the new facts that...

> "The magistrate is a paid professional man subject to a distant board and the village constable is superseded by a police officer from a central board and when schoolmasters and schoolbooks are submitted to the government of some foreign authority."

He clearly saw, as if by second sight, our whole degenerate culture of OFSTEDs and regulatory bodies.

The gradual weakening of religious authority in Newman's time produced a much more powerful but godless authority and, worst of all, a sort of merging of the true function of the church with a burgeoning secular bureaucracy. He commented:

"A whirl of business is always unfavourable to depth and accuracy of religious views."

And, on a related subject about which I feel increasingly rueful as the pile of brown envelopes from the diocesan office gets ever taller:

"There is now too much unavoidable secular business in parish work."

In our times the church has adopted in their entirety all the paraphernalia of secular bureaucracies and management jargon. When I was vicar of my first parish thirty years ago, the Annual Diocesan Return was a single sheet of paper on which I was asked to record the number of baptisms, marriages and funerals, how many people were on the Electoral Roll and how many had attended church at Christmas and Easter. I could complete it in ten minutes over my morning coffee. Nowadays the Return is parcel a foot thick and some of the questions are so abstruse and arcane that it seems designed to be impossible to complete fully. Newman complains that this trend began in his day.

He also saw that secularisation would result in the trivialisation of public life and discourse:

"Every quarter of a year, every month, every day, there must be a supply for the gratification of the public of new and luminous theories. There is a demand for a reckless originality of thought and a sparkling plausibility of argument. They can give no better guarantee for the philosophical truth of their principles than their popularity at the moment and their happy conformity in ethical character to the age which admires them."

This is the horrific vision of a nation which has lost touch with God, lost all belief in him. It is a nation therefore which has lost its true perspective, lost its soul. And a perspectiveless world has no alternative but to say that all ideas and thoughts are of the same value; to babble on about unconnected processes as if they were linked; to become *non-judgemental;* that is undiscriminating, unintelligent and finally amoral. Where there is no perspective, no order of values, then the notions of good and bad, and indeed of truth itself, no longer have any meaning for us.

The trend of liberalism is progressive reductionism. Newman saw this and he understood that the general trend of liberalism implies a constant retreat. He said,

"Let all who are inclined to retreat ask themselves whether they contemplate any position in their rear at which they propose to make a stand."

Because Newman was a poet, he found ways of expressing the church's dogmas memorably in verses that people can learn easily and call to remembrance when they are needed:

"Firmly I believe and truly, God is three and God is one;
And I next acknowledge duly, manhood taken by the Son."

And poetry is a better teacher than prose. By rhythm and sensual enchantment, poetry implants meaning more deeply within us that prose ever can. We might say that poetry to prose is as the icon to the ordinary picture. Poetry embodies its meaning and becomes a literary imitation of the Incarnation: words made flesh. Here, for instance, is Newman's summary of the Christian faith in four lines. It is as easy to learn as *Jack and Jill went up the hill:*

"O loving wisdom of our God, when all was sin and shame,
A second Adam to the fight and to the rescue came
And that a higher gift than grace should flesh and blood refine;
God's presence and his very self, and essence all divine."

If we memorise those lines we have, so to speak, the Christian faith in our back pocket. And when he was seasick on a ship on the Mediterranean at night he wrote verses which quickly became known and loved throughout England. These words are so memorable, so treasured, because they embody true Christian psychology, the condition of the soul utterly dependent on God not merely in some abstracted and everlasting stream of consciousness, but from one second to the next:

"Lead kindly light amidst the encircling gloom, lead thou me on;
The night is dark and I am far from home, lead thou me on.
Keep thou my feet; I do not ask to see
The distant scene; one step enough for me."

As a writer of English prose, Newman was among the greatest. He was a competent and resourceful poet and the most luminously intelligent theologian of the 19th century. As with St Augustine, we see his spiritual depth most of all in his sermons and prayers. When you feel the need for comfort and reassurance, when life goes hard, when the night is dark and you are far from home, remember that God loves you and will never forsake you and remember this:

"O Lord, support us all the day long, until the shadows lengthen and the evening comes, and the busy world is hushed, and the fever of life is over, and our work is done. Then in thy mercy grant us a safe lodging and a holy rest, and peace at the last. Amen."

Chapter Four

G.K. Chesterton (1874–1936)

Chesterton was born in London where he attended St Paul's School and studied at The Slade. He was from the beginning of his career a prolific essayist and journalist for magazines such as *The Bookman, The Illustrated London News* and *The Speaker.* From 1925 he published his own magazine, *G.K.'s Weekly.* His first books were collections of poetry: *The Wild Knight* (1900) and *Greybeards at Play* in the same year. In 1904 he published the brilliantly original and surreal anti-imperial satire *The Napoleon of Notting Hill.* He was married to Frances Blogg to whom he was deeply devoted.

He also produced perceptive studies of Browning, Dickens and Stevenson. While still an Anglican, he published in 1909 *Orthodoxy* – a persuasive and very entertaining defence of the Christian Faith. In 1911 he introduced his eccentric fictional detective in *The Innocence of Father Brown.* In 1922 he became a Roman Catholic and produced lives of St Thomas Aquinas and St Francis of Assisi. His *Autobiography* was published posthumously in 1936.

Chesterton was physically large and his witty, mischievous character ensured he was always larger than life and one of the most popular and celebrated writers of his day.

In 1904, Chesterton wrote as follows in the *Daily News:*

"The other day I was nearly arrested by two excited policemen in Yorkshire. At the moment in question, I was throwing a big Swedish knife at a tree, practising (alas without success) that useful trick of knife-throwing by which men murder each other in Stevenson's romances. Suddenly the forest was full of two policemen. They asked what the knife was, why I was throwing it, what my address was, trade, religion, opinions on the Japanese War, name of favourite cat and so on. The tree was none the less damaged, even though it may reflect with a dark pride that it was wounded by a gentleman connected with the Liberal press."

That is a piece of quintessential Chesterton: it is amusing; it is a story that holds our interest; but above all it paints a vivid picture of a real flesh-and-blood scene. This is the first thing to be said about Chesterton and all his works. He was a huge, thoroughly incarnated man with nothing tenuous or theoretical about him. This is what makes his writing so clear and convincing. Even when he is writing about philosophy or the theology of St Thomas Aquinas, his words are, as it were, set in stone. It takes great skill and practice to think and write like that, for it reveals a man who has really got inside his subject and from there he represents it with startling persuasiveness to the reader. Like God, he creates a whole world and puts his stamp on it. The description *Chestertonian* is appropriate.

He was captivated by the concept of *making*, an activity which he regarded as being of the very highest calling He said:

"All the modern talk about the necessary dullness of domesticity and the degrading drudgery that only has to make puddings and pies. *Only* to make things! There is no greater good to be said of God himself than that He makes things. Religion is a practical thing – like gardening."

Asked to account for his early success as a journalist, he said that the art of comic success in journalism

"...is to write an article for *Church Times* and another for *Sporting Times* and put them in the wrong envelopes. "

All his writings are engaging but one of the most exuberant, and typically self-deprecating is his *Autobiography* which he begins:

"I was born of respectable but honest parents: that is in a world where the word *respectability* was not yet exclusively a term of abuse, but retained some dim philological connection with the idea of being respected."

The ironical flavour is there from the start: it is quintessentially Chestertonian that he does not say,

"...respectable *and* honest parents" but "respectable *but* honest parents." – as if there were almost something unrespectable about being respectable. This is an example of his famous paradoxical style which he used to great effect in his Christian apologetics. The usual meaning of *paradox* suggests contradiction but it is illuminating to see that its derivation is from *para* – by the side of – and *doxa,* the Greek for *glory*. So the most mystical and glorious things are unsurprisingly mistaken for contradictions.

Chesterton was always affectionately but tellingly subversive of *respectability* and of the rigid social structure of his day. He tells a tale about a lady in his family who went to live with a friend. During the friend's absence, she was waited upon by what Chesterton describes as,

"...a sort of superior servant."

In this little tale, Chesterton lays his finger precisely on what class differences are all about:

"The lady had got it into her head that the servant cooked her own meals separately, whereas the servant was equally fixed on the policy of eating what was left over from the lady's meals. The servant sent up for breakfast five rashers of bacon, which was more than the lady wanted. But the lady had another fixed freak of conscience common in the ladies of the period. She thought nothing should be wasted, and could not see that even a thing consumed is wasted if it is not wanted. So she ate the five rashers and the hungry, disappointed servant sent up seven rashers. The lady paled a little, but followed the path of duty and ate them all. The servant, beginning to feel that she too would like a little breakfast, sent up nine or ten rashers. The lady, rallying all her powers, charged at them with her head down and swept them from the field. And so it went on, owing to the polite silence between the two social classes. I dare not think how it ended. The logical conclusion would seem to be that the servant starved and the lady burst."

He was brought up by his respectable parents to speak properly. And at an early age he knew the power he could derive from disobeying his parents in so respectable a matter:

"About the age of three or four, I screamed for a hat hanging on a peg, and at last in convulsions of fury uttered the awful words, 'If you don't give me it, I'll say 'at'!'"

Even in the middle of these wry anecdotes he shows wisdom in a well-chosen sentence. Here for example is a profound literary insight:

"I knew pages of Shakespeare's blank verse without a notion of the meaning of most of it – which is perhaps the right way to begin to appreciate verse."

How different from the modern prejudice in education which always seeks to put understanding before acquaintance. But Chesterton knew, as C.H. Sisson remarked,

"We learn by rote before we learn by light."

And it is symptomatic of our mechanistic, morbidly calculating world view that we prefer these days to say *by rote* instead of the older and more affectionate *by heart*. Rote-learning replaces heart-learning as a prelude to its being dismissed by modern minded educational bureaucrats as a worthless activity compared with their preferred *self-expression*. But *by heart* suggests something that is lovable, heartfelt, and so consolidates the act of learning as a process in which the pupil might find pleasure – even joy.

Chesterton's insight into how we best learn to appreciate poetry is immediately followed by a scintillating literary-psychological comparison:

> "Dr Jekyll and Mr Hyde is a double triumph: it has the outside excitement that belongs to Conan Doyle with the inside excitement that belongs to Henry James."

Then an acerbic political insight:

> "The Whig aristocrats who made the Revolution – and incidentally their own fortunes..."

A man with strong family ties, Chesterton has fond recollections of his grandfather, but they are not just fond recollections, they are very moving spiritual insights:

> "People were criticising the General Thanksgiving in the Prayer Book, and remarking that a good many people have very little reason to be thankful for their creation. And the old man, who was then so old that he hardly ever spoke at all, said suddenly out of his silence, *I should thank God for my creation even if I knew I was a lost soul.*"

Still in connection with his grandfather, he finds a gentle way to rebuke humbug:

> "A solemn friend of my grandfather used to go for walks on Sunday carrying a prayer book, without the least intention of going to church. And he calmly defended it with uplifted hand, *I do it Chessie as an example to others.*"

He was particularly good on the hypocrisy of this sort of peculiarly *spiritual* humbug:

"The well-known S.C. Hall, the Spiritualist, cleared himself with an eloquence which some found too sublime to be convincing. *How can I be said to resemble Pecksniff?* said this worthy man to my father. *You know me, the world knows me. The world knows that I have devoted my life to the good of others, that I have lived a pure and exalted life devoted to the highest duties and ideals, that I have always sought to set an example of truth, of justice, of probity, of purity and of public virtue. What resemblance can there be between me and Pecksniff?*"

His surreal sense of self-deprecation is never far away, as for instance when he speaks of his wedding day:

"I stopped on the way to church to drink a glass of milk in one shop and to buy a revolver with cartridges in another. Some have seen these as singular wedding presents for a bridegroom to give himself: and if the bride had known less of him, I suppose she might have fancied that he was a suicide or a murderer, or, worst of all, a teetotaller."

This amusing autobiography is speckled with acute judge-ments of a very serious sort – of what has come to be regarded as the wit and wisdom of G.K. Chesterton – but the first thing to notice is that he didn't, as it were, write books of wit and then write some other books of wisdom: the wit and wisdom are always combined. For instance, speaking of those enthusiasts who are forever instructing us about our solemn duty towards distant foreign parts, he says,

"The sect that did so much to liberate Africa, the Clapham Sect – that did so little to liberate Clapham."

We notice that this tendency to sentimentalise affairs has not gone away. In our own day this pretended concern with events thousands of miles away, coupled as it is with a profound ignorance of what is under one's nose, has become a political epidemic. It is often those who speak so earnestly about the need to save the planet, or at least to save Africa, reveal themselves impotent even to save their village post-office. Again it is the preference for something which, by definition, can only be contemplated in the abstract over the tangible realities of what is close to home; those things with which a person might reasonably be expected to engage. Chesterton was clearer about this than many so called *experts* on foreign policy today:

> "The supposed duty towards humanity in general may often take the form of a choice which is personal or even pleasurable. That duty may be a hobby. It may even be a dissipation...."

(We think perhaps of Bob Geldoff and rock concerts to save starving Africans whose real enemies are not, after all, the forces of a cruel nature or climate but the treachery and irresponsibility of their own rulers).

> "...We may work in the East End because we are peculiarly fitted to work in the East End, or because we think we are; we may fight for the cause of international peace because we are very fond of fighting. The most monstrous martyrdom, the most repulsive experience, may be the result of choice or a kind of taste. We may be so made as to be particularly fond of lunatics or specially interested in leprosy. We may love Negroes because they are black or German socialists because they are pedantic. But we have to love our neighbour because he is *there* – a much more alarming reason for a much more serious operation. Our neighbour is the example of humanity which is actually given to us. Precisely because he may be anybody, he is everybody. He is a symbol because he is an accident."

It is the sheer enjoyment with which he exposes humbug that is so impressive:

"Socialists were inconsistent in saying that a peasant has no right to a field, but a peasantry has a right to an oilfield."

I think this nose for sniffing out hypocrisy is something he caught from Dickens. He says of the *bien pensants* of his day:

"If the barricades went up in our streets and the poor became masters, I think the priests would escape. I fear the gentlemen would; but I believe the gutters would be simply running with the blood of the philanthropists."

Indeed, of Dickens himself he says,

"The only elementary ethical truth that is essential in the study of Dickens is that he had broad or universal sympathies in a sense totally unknown to the social reformers who wallow in such phrases."

The humour overflows, and the paradoxical Chesterton knew that the best jokes are about the most serious subjects and so his jokes often concern morality and religion. Next time we come across a coterie of Hampstead Buddhists, spiritualised vegetarians and enthusiasts for the inner light, we might call to mind Chesterton's demolition of the essential amorality of this outlook:

"A sort of Theosophist said to me, *Good and evil, truth and falsehood, folly and wisdom are only aspects of the same upward movement of the universe.* Even at that stage it occurred to me to ask, *Supposing there is no difference between good and bad, or between false and true, what is the difference between up and down?*"

He could be very explicit about the relationship between the most sacred things and our sense of the ridiculous. When he was accused of being frivolous about religious matters, he replied very pointedly:

"The people who really take the name of the Lord in vain are the clergymen themselves. The thing that is fundamentally and really frivolous is not a careless joke. The thing which is fundamentally and really frivolous is a careless solemnity."

He anticipates our own age of non-judgementalism and the political correctness which celebrates the fallacy of claiming on the one hand that all judgements are relative, that there are no absolute moral concepts – except the absolute of universal human rights:

"A whole generation has been taught to talk nonsense at the top of its voice about having *a right to life* and *a right to experience* and *a right to happiness*. The lucid thinkers who talk like this generally wind up their assertion of all these extraordinary rights by saying that there is no such thing as right and wrong."

In fact for once Chesterton understates his case, for actually the people who are most enthusiastic about all the multifarious sorts of rights are always and everywhere the selfsame people who deny the reality of absolute moral values. He would surely regard our banal modern service books and the scarcely-veiled blasphemy which constitutes all this capering about, cuddling and back-slapping in church as things beyond even his capacious powers of satire.

It is strange to find that those who harp on the notion of liberty so ceaselessly often turn out to be determinists. But how can one even begin to talk about freedom and liberty in a world which is materialistically programmed? Chesterton spent much of his life refuting determinism, but with characteristic verve:

"There could be no better example than this queer appearance of the determinist as a demagogue, shouting to a mob of millions that no man ought to be blamed for anything he did because it was all heredity and environment. Logically, it would stop a man in the act of saying, *Thank you* to somebody for passing the mustard. For how could he be praised for passing the mustard, if he could not be blamed for not passing the mustard? If determinism makes no difference, why should the determinist thunder from his pulpit about the difference it makes?"

In a related area, he probably saw Darwin's evolutionary biology as possibly true, but by no means the whole truth:

"So many poets after Darwin try desperately to write about machinery: touching which nobody has yet disputed the Argument from Design. No Darwin has yet maintained that motor cars began as scraps of metal, of which most happened to be scrapped; or that only those cars which had grown a carburettor by accident survived the struggle for life in Piccadilly."

Chesterton was a large man with a large heart and he valued friendship as much as life itself. He gives us many affectionate reflections on his literary contemporaries. Here, for example, he describes how once when Henry James was staying at Rye, Chesterton's boozy friends, led by Hilaire Belloc, dropped in. They were very scruffy, having run out of money in France and been obliged to walk all the way from Dover:

"Henry James had left America because he loved Europe, and all that was meant by England or France; the gentry, the gallantry, the traditions of lineage and locality, the life that had been lived beneath old portraits in oak-panelled rooms. And there on the other side of the tea-table was Europe, was the old thing that made France and England, the posterity of the English squires and the French soldiers; ragged, unshaven, shouting for beer, shameless above all shades of poverty and wealth; sprawling, indifferent, secure. And what looked across at it was still the Puritan refinement of Boston; and the space it looked across was wider than the Atlantic."

And he defined Henry James' literary style in a single phrase when he spoke of his friend as being,

"...in an agony of verbal precision"

There is a revelatory book of criticism by Chesterton called *The Victorian Age in Literature* in which he offers the most striking judgements on his contemporaries and near contemporaries. What appeals most strongly about Chesterton's literary judgements is that they are usually devoid of any bitterness or animus, but there are exceptions. For example:

"In Aubrey Beardlsey there is a certain brief mood, a certain narrow aspect of life which he renders to the imagination rightly. It is mostly felt under white, deathly lights in Piccadilly, with the black hollow of heaven behind shiny hats or painted faces: a horrible impression that all mankind are masks. This being the thing that Beardsley could express (and the only thing he could express), it is the solemn and awful fact that he was set down to illustrate Malory's *Morte d'Arthur.* There is no need to say more; taste in the artist's sense must have been utterly dead. They might as well have employed Burne-Jones to illustrate *Martin Chuzzlewit.*"

Decadence and despair in art and literature were as common in Chesterton's day as they are in ours. And it is just as misplaced. Who are decadent nihilists such as Beckett to exult in their sardonic prose attitudes of mind and heart that the biblical prophets have been warning us against for millennia? As Chesterton says of the atheist Swinburne's presumptuous pessimism:

"He hurls at the priest the assertion that all flesh is grass and that life is sorrow and in this he really lays himself open to the restrained answer from the man of God, *So I have ventured, on various occasions, to remark.*"

His greatness as a critic is revealed by the fact that it is precisely when he is being most jocular that his pot-shots are so deadly accurate:

> "We feel it is a disgrace to a man like Ruskin when he says, with a solemn visage, that building in iron is ugly and unreal, but that the weightiest objection to it is that there is no mention of iron in the Bible. We feel as if he had just said that he could find no hairbrushes in the Book of the Prophet Habakkuk."

He enjoyed and endured half a lifetime's sparring with H.G.Wells with whom he was hardly compatible. But his remarks about Wells – like his frequent criticisms of Shaw – are always generous and affectionate. This makes the judgments even more telling:

> "Whenever I met Wells, he seemed to me to be coming from somewhere, rather than going anywhere. He always had been a Liberal, or had been a Fabian, or had been a friend of Henry James or Bernard Shaw. And he was so often nearly right, that his movements irritated me like the sight of someone's hat being perpetually washed up by the sea, and never touching the shore..."

So the effect is for the very idea of Wells to be forever implanted in the reader's mind with that picture of the seashore and the melancholy hat – *never touching the shore.* He goes on:

> "But I think Wells thought that the object of opening the mind is simply opening the mind. Whereas I am incurably convinced that the object of opening the mind, as of opening the mouth, is to shut it again on something solid."

When we come to Wells and Chesterton – at least in the years before Well's change of temper and his great terminal depression – we are faced with the chasm between the utopian optimist Wells and the realist Chesterton. Nowhere is this more obvious than in attitudes towards the First World War. Chesterton thus satirised the sentimentalists who thought that the mere scale of the conflict ought to result in some future paradise:

> "To tell a soldier defending his country that it is *the War That Will End War* is exactly like telling a workman, naturally rather reluctant to do his day's work, that it is *the Work That Will End Work.* We never promised to put a final end to all war or all work or all worry. We only said that we were bound to endure something very bad because the alternative was something worse. In short, we said what every man on the defensive has to say. Mr Brown is attacked by a burglar and manages to save his life and property. It is absurd to turn round on him and say, *After all, what has come out of the battle in the back-garden. It is the same old Septimus Brown, with the same face, the same trousers, the same temper a little uncertain at breakfast, the same taste for telling the anecdote about the bookmaker at Brighton.* It is absurd to complain that Mr Brown has not been turned into a Greek god merely by being bashed on the head by a burglar."

And it was during that First Great War – in 1916 – Chesterton showed remarkable prescience about the even greater horror that would shortly follow it:

> "Idolatry; a dehumanised seriousness. The men of the forest are already building upon a mountain the empty throne of the Superman."

Journalism, treatises on distributist economics, poems, the satirical far-sighted comic novel *The Napoleon of Notting Hill,* the entertaining and ingenious Father Brown stories: in such encompassing virtuosity he showed himself to be one of the brightest literary lights of his age. But the centre of his motivation was the Christian religion and its defence. We find the flavour of his ingenious and persuasive apologetics in his *Orthodoxy*. He had not at this stage in his life read St Thomas Aquinas, but he begins with a statement that might have been penned by the Angelic Doctor himself:

> "A man was meant to be doubtful about himself, but undoubting about the truth; this has been exactly reversed. Nowadays the part of a man that a man really does assert is exactly the part he ought not to assert – himself. The part he doubts is exactly the part he ought not to doubt – the Divine Reason."

This is an early warning to our age and our obsession with self-affirming and the narcissistic cult of self-esteem. Like St Thomas, Chesterton insists that there is in the world objective reason and order which goes beyond subjectivity or psychological sensations. There is a truth which is not merely what I might consider true *for me.* It is Chesterton's purpose in *Orthodoxy* to expose the pattern of this truth, and he does so by considering and demolishing popular fallacies. These fallacies have not changed much from his day to ours. For example, the creed of materialism was then, as now, regarded as a common sense outlook which liberates men from the tyranny of religious dogma, but, he says,

> "When materialism leads men to complete fatalism, as it generally does, it is quite idle to pretend that it is in any sense a liberating force. It is absurd to say that you are especially advancing freedom when you only use free thought to destroy freewill."

Chesterton exposed the prejudice – and it is nothing but a prejudice – that Christianity and the miracle stories of the New Testament have been undermined by science and the higher criticism of the liberal school in theology, and that consequently the only plausible intellectual stance is materialism. But he counters:

"In truth the notion that we are *free* to deny miracles has nothing to do with the evidence for or against them. It is a lifeless, verbal prejudice of which the life and beginning was not in the freedom of thought, but simply in the dogma of materialism. The man of the nineteenth century did not disbelieve in the Resurrection because his liberal Christianity allowed him to doubt it. He disbelieved in it because his very strict materialism did not allow him to believe it."

That is to say, materialism as a doctrine is not the result of a sustained process of thought which examines all the alternatives to materialism and finds them wanting; it is simply an assumption – what Chesterton rightly calls a prejudice. A near target is the notion that truth can be obliterated by the mere passage of time, that it can somehow become out of date. For example that jibe of Bultmann's to the effect that one cannot believe the miracles and the Resurrection *in an age of electric light and the wireless.* Scientific theories, by contrast *do* become out of date because every new scientific theory is born out of the falsification of its predecessor. *The most beautiful hypothesis slain by a single brute fact.* But the Creeds are not scientific statements. Chesterton says:

"An imbecile habit has arisen in modern controversy of saying that such and such a creed can be held in one age but cannot be held in another. Some dogma, we are told, was credible in the twelfth century, but it is not credible in the twentieth. You might as well say that a certain philosophy can be believed on Mondays, but cannot be believed on Tuesdays."

In fact, he says:

"The spike of dogma fitted exactly into the hole in the world."

This means that, although religious truth does not derive from subjective experience, it is confirmed by everyday experience. By religious truth, Chesterton explicitly means Christian truth. In what would today be considered monstrously politically-incorrect, he dares to say that the eastern religions and the fashionable esotericisms of what, in the West, is now called *spirituality* are dead ends. For instance:

> "I know a man who has such a passion for proving that he will have no personal existence after death that he falls back on the position that he has no personal existence now. He invokes Buddhism and says that all souls fade into each other: in order to prove that he cannot go to heaven, he proves that he cannot go to Hartlepool."

Chesterton always regarded free-floating *spirituality* as a most dangerous preoccupation:

> "By insisting specially on the immanence of God and the inner light, we get introspection, self-isolation, quietism, social indifference – Tibet. By insisting specially, as Christian doctrine does, on the transcendence of God, we get wonder, curiosity, moral and political adventure, righteous indignation – Christendom."

In her biography of Chesterton, Maisie Ward relates how in 1932 he asked Dorothy Collins to go to London and *get me some books.* She asked him, *What books?* And he replied, *I don't know...*

She wrote therefore to their mutual friend Father O'Connor and from him got a list of classic and more recent books on St Thomas. Chesterton flipped them rapidly through, which is, says Dorothy, the only way she ever saw him read and then dictated to her his book about Aquinas without ever referring to them again. Of the book she thought,

> "What will the experts say? Of the verdict of the greatest of them, we were not long left in doubt. Etienne Gilson,

who has given two of the most famous of philosophical lecture series – the Gifford Lectures at Aberdeen and the William James Lectures at Harvard – said, *Chesterton makes one despair. I have been studying St Thomas all my life and I could never have written such a book. I consider it as being without possible comparison the best book ever written on St Thomas. Nothing short of genius can account for such an achievement."*

Genius aided and abetted by grace, no doubt.

Chesterton succeeded brilliantly in his aim to offer a popular understanding of some of the most profound philosophy ever written. And, as always in Chesterton, the result is exciting. To start at the beginning:

"Perhaps it would be best to say, *There is an Is*. That is as much monkish credulity as St Thomas asks of us at the start. Very few unbelievers start by asking us to believe so little. And yet upon this sharp pinpoint of reality, he rears by long logical processes that have never really been successfully overthrown, the whole cosmic system of Christendom."

He proceeds to elaborate Aquinas' First Cause argument:

"There is always something unthinkable about the whole evolutionary cosmos, because it is something coming out of nothing; an ever-increasing flood of water pouring out of an empty jug. In a word, the world does not explain itself, and cannot do so merely by continuing to expand itself. But anyway, it is absurd for the evolutionist to complain that it is unthinkable for an admittedly unthinkable God to make everything out of nothing; and then pretend it is more thinkable that nothing should turn itself into everything...

"Most thinkers on realising the apparent mutability of being, have really forgotten their own realisation of being and believed only in the mutability. They cannot even say that a thing changes into another thing; for them there is no instant in the process at which it is a thing at all. It is only a change...

"To sum up: the reality of things, the mutability of things, the diversity of things, and all such other things that can be attributed to things, is followed carefully by the medieval philosopher without losing touch with the original point of the reality. There is no space in this book to specify the thousand steps of thought by which he shows that he is right. But the point is that, even apart from being right, he is real...Even the doubts and difficulties about reality have driven him to believe in more reality rather than less. The deceitfulness of things which has had so sad an effect on so many sages, has almost a contrary effect on this sage. If things deceive us, it is by being more real than they seem."

There is an Is. That is, there is something. And, if there is something, how does it come about that there is something? Nothing that we can point to in the world is the author of its own existence. There must be a Creator, Something – or rather Someone – who is not dependent or contingent in this way. Aquinas was re-phrasing Aristotle's doctrine of the Unmoved Mover in the service of Christian apologetics.

Every age is tempted to think that its own preoccupations and problems are peculiar to itself – as if the intellectual life of a civilisation were something invented entire and anew by every generation. But in his book *The Everlasting Man*, Chesterton describes how the most dangerous heresies constantly recur; and against these he sets the extraordinary persistence of the Christian Faith:

"At least five times, with the Arian and the Albigensian, with the Humanist sceptic, after Voltaire and after Darwin, the Faith has to all appearances gone to the dogs. In each of these five cases, it was the dog that died."

The church is the guardian of civilisation. He says,

> "If the Church had not entered the world, it seems probable that Europe would be now very much what Asia is now."

But, as he says, the struggle against the forces of darkness, pessimism, epistemological and moral relativism continues; and it depends on men and women with their God-given freewill constantly choosing to believe what is right (and even to try to do what is right) and to reject what is wrong.
Chesterton says,

> "Mankind is always at the crossroads; but at the crossroads there is, thank God, the Cross."

And, towards the end of *The Everlasting Man,* Chesterton protests against the ill-judged progressivism which seems especially to afflict our times:

> "One of the ablest agnostics of the age once asked me whether I thought mankind grew better or grew worse or remained the same. He was confident that these alternatives covered all possibilities. He did not see that it only covered patterns and not pictures; processes and not stories. I asked him whether he thought Mr Smith of Golders Green got better or worse or remained exactly the same between the age of thirty and forty. It then seemed to dawn on him that it would rather depend on Mr Smith and how he chose to go on. But it had never occurred to him that it might depend on how mankind chose to go on; and that its course was not a straight line or an upward or downward curve, but a track like that of a man across a valley going where he liked and stopping where he chose, going into church or falling drunk in a ditch. The life of man is a story; an adventure story; and in our vision the same is true even of the story of God."

His little poem *The Donkey* perfectly encapsulates Chesterton's gift for expressing the deepest things in small gestures of apparent whimsy:

> "When fishes flew and forests walked
> And figs grew upon thorn,
> Some moment when the moon was blood
> Then surely I was born.
>
> "With monstrous head and sickening cry
> And ears like errant wings,
> The devil's walking parody
> On all four-footed things.
>
> "The tattered outlaw of the earth,
> Of ancient crooked will;
> Starve, scourge, deride me: I am dumb,
> I keep my secret still.
>
> "Fools! For I also had my hour;
> One far fierce hour and sweet:
> There was a shout about my ears
> And palms before my feet."

Chapter 5

T.E. Hulme (1883–1917)

Hulme was born at Gratton Hall, Endon, Staffordshire, the son of Thomas the son of a gentleman farmer. He was highly intelligent and energetic from an early age. Michael Roberts said of him:

> "Even at the top-spinning age, he was engrossed in a book about gyrostatics."

He attended Newcastle-under-Lyme High School and in 1902 he went up to St John's College, Cambridge to read mathematics. He was sent down in 1904 after rowdy and bawdy behaviour on the night after the annual university boat race and a riot in a theatre. He was so popular among the undergraduates that he was sent off with a huge and flamboyant mock funeral. Although he regained his place at St John's, he was dismissed again after a scandal involving a girl from Roedean. He resumed his studies at University College, London, then travelled in Canada and spent time in Brussels learning European languages.

Some time around 1907 Hulme developed an amateur interest in philosophy and he translated works by Henri Bergson and Georges Sorel's *Reflections on Violence*. The most important influences on his thought at this time were Bergson and later Wilhelm Worringer (1881–1965), the German art historian and critic. Hulme took a particular interest in Worringer's *Abstraktion und Einfühlung* (*Abstraction and Empathy*, 1908).

He discovered an ability to compose sparse and extraordinarily vivid poems and became secretary of *The Poets' Club* which was frequented by Edmund Gosse and Henry Newbolt. At *The Poets' Club* he met the prominent modernists Ezra

Pound and F. S. Flint. In 1908 Hulme delivered his paper *A Lecture on Modern Poetry* at the club. Hulme's own poems *The Complete Poetical Works of T.E. Hulme* was published in *The New Age* in 1912, consisting of only five poems – a sixth appeared later. He has a claim to be the earliest Imagist poet, and his manifesto for that style greatly influenced Pound and, through his literary and social criticism, T. S. Eliot. Hulme's writings strongly impressed Wyndham Lewis and he wrote for Lewis' magazine *Blast.* As an art critic, he championed the work of Jacob Epstein and David Bomberg and became a friend of Gaudier-Brzeska.

Hulme volunteered as an artilleryman in 1914, and served with the Royal Marine Artillery in France and Belgium. He continued to write for *The New Age*, and wrote *War Notes* under the pen name "North Staffs", and *A Notebook*, which contains some of his most acute critical writing. He was wounded in 1916. Back at the front in 1917, he was killed by a shell at Oostduinkerke near Nieuwpoort in West Flanders.

The best way to catch the flavour of the man is through his intense poetry. Here is his *Autumn*:

"A touch of cold in the Autumn night
I walked abroad,
And saw the ruddy moon lean over a hedge
Like a red-faced farmer.
I did not stop to speak, but nodded;
And round about were the wistful stars
With white faces like town children."

This next one is titled *Above the Dock*:

"Above the quiet dock at midnight,
Tangled in the tall mast's corded height,
Hangs the moon. What seemed so far away
Is but a child's balloon, forgotten after play."

What we have in these short poems is the immediate presentation of reality by means of striking images. Most of the other poetry being written at the beginning of the last century was decadent Romanticism, post-Swinburne sham antique – what Eliot called in another context the attempt *to summon the spectre of a rose and follow an antique drum.* Hulme's aim was for a poetry that was hard-edged, without frills or floweriness, but packed full of memorable metaphors – *the stars with white faces like town children,* the moon a balloon. He believed that the fresh metaphor, by bringing together vivid images, provided the reader with an original view of reality. And it was from Hulme that Pound derived his doctrine that *the image is the perfect symbol* – that is, the poet should resist the temptation to pile words on words in the belief that thereby his *meaning* will be intensified : in fact, the opposite will happen. Pound said,

"Do not say *dim lands of peace.*"

Or, as R.G. Collingwood remarked,

"If you wish to evoke something which is truly dreadful, don't say *It was dreadful.*"

On this issue, A.R. Jones wrote of Hulme's intention:

"Hulme clings to the Aristotelian belief that the greatest of all excellences is to be happy in the use of metaphor, for it is the quick discernment of resemblances which is the mark of the poet."

Similarly, C.H. Sisson said of Hulme's poems:

"There is such concentration that one feels one has the complete content of the mind at the moment of the poem. Each poem of Hulme's is a sort of instantaneous carving out of reality with a knife".

Sisson adds:

"A man walking on the sea shore has to have something in his head. The romantic is so to speak a holiday-maker with vague thoughts of luxurious beauty. The classic is a man no less serious than the fisherman mending his nets. His preoccupations do not leave him. He does not turn aside for beauty. No good writer does. In a sense, Hulme's distinction between classic and romantic is merely the distinction between good writing and bad."

This is a stricture by no means rendered superfluous in our day when art is regarded as a branch of the entertainments and amusements industry and its purpose is usually to stir emotions so trivial they had better not been stirred at all. Hulme's doctrine of metaphor was that shocking conjunctions create new intuitions. He said,

"Images are born in poetry, they are used in prose and finally they die a long and lingering death in journalists' English".

And he predicted that,

"In modern poetry we should expect a revival of classicism."

But this is not a return to Alexander Pope. He added,

"When it does come, we may not even regard it as classical."

And that of course is just what happened when, a few years later, Eliot published *Prufrock* and *The Waste Land*. Critics steeped in the Romantic tradition imagined that Eliot's purpose must have been to declare himself a leader of the *avant garde*, and that the classical aspects and allusions – including the mischievous footnotes – were part of a clever joke. Nothing could be further from the truth. Eliot's classicism was deliberate.

Hulme altogether despised Romantic poetry:

"I object to the sloppiness which doesn't consider that a poem is a poem unless it is moaning or whining about something. There is a general tendency to think that verse means little else than the expression of unsatisfied emotion:

Golden lads and girls all must,
As chimney-sweepers come to dust

"The Romantic would never have used the word *lads*. He would have to write *golden youth* and take up the thing at least a couple of notes in pitch."

Famously he offered his definition:

"Romanticism is spilt religion."

Metaphor is used to try to get at a reality that is always transcendent: God certainly, but also the world of experience which is never perfectly describable. Reality just *is* and it can be described and represented successfully only in briefly illuminating expressions and images – if at all. Hulme said:

"Language is recalcitrant matter. The process of poetic invention is that of gradually making solid the castles in the air. At last I come to think that all expression is vulgar, that only the unexpressed and silent is real."

This is an extremely mystical interpretation of experience and it echoes St Paul's talk of seeing through a glass darkly and all the other evocations, types and shadows in religious imagery. Hulme never met his contemporary, the philosopher Wittgenstein, but he would have agreed strongly with Wittgenstein's famous statement at the end of *Tractatus Logico Philosophicus*:

"What we cannot speak about, we must commit to silence."

It is a double coincidence that both men were at Cambridge and later in the trenches – where they fought on opposing sides.

Poetry, Hulme thought, is the restless attempt to portray what is ultimately transcendent. And this is only ever achieved sporadically, momentarily by the vivid image which is the true icon, but not such an icon as one can affix to the wall: these images are like lightning flashes which strike and illuminate for a second before they are gone. He said:

"Verse is pedestrian, taking you over the ground. Prose is a train which delivers you at a destination."

The highest form of language is poetry because:

"It always endeavours to arrest you and to make you continuously see a physical thing, to prevent you gliding through an abstract process. It chooses fresh epithets and fresh metaphors, not so much because they are new and we are tired of the old, but because the old ceases to convey a physical thing and becomes abstract counters. Prose is the museum where the dead images of verse are preserved."

Hulme's desire to portray experience through images, striking metaphors and analogies, is a pre-echo of Eliot's description of the poet's task which is

"...to purify the dialect of the tribe."

Or as Ezra Pound taught young poets:

"Make it new!"

Hulme's preference for striking images in poetry was paralleled in his opinions about painting and sculpture. He said:

"Renaissance art we may call *vital* art in that it depends on pleasure in the reproduction of human and natural forms. Byzantine art is the exact contrary of this. There is nothing vital in it. The emotion you get from it is not a pleasure in the reproduction of natural or human life. The disgust with the trivial and accidental characteristics of living shapes, the searching after an austerity, a perfection and a rigidity which vital things can never have, leads here to the use of forms which can almost be called *geometrical.* Man is subordinate to certain absolute values; there is no delight in the human form, leading to its natural reproduction; it is always distorted to fit into the more abstract forms which convey an intense religious emotion."

Again Jones commented:

"Hulme feels a strong sympathy for the art of Donatello, Michelangelo and Marlowe; but he maintains that their humanism contains the seeds of errors that culminated in Rousseau and Romanticism."

Hulme reviewed Epstein's controversial 1913 exhibition and Epstein said his review was,

"The sanest article ever written about me."

In this review, Hulme used characteristically violent language against Epstein's severest critic, calling him,

"...a charlatan...a little Cockney intellect...stupid and childish...the most appropriate way of dealing with him would be a little personal violence."

This was entirely in line with his conviction that the strength of a belief is measurable by the extent one is prepared to fight for it:

"This is what I call a real, vital interest in literature: it has to affect the body."

Hulme rejoiced to see in modern art the breakup of the Renaissance humanistic tradition which was art with the human form and human aspirations at the centre – as you might say, the artistic version of the contemporary Cartesianism which begins with the *I* of *I think, therefore I am*. Of this anthropocentric, humanistic view, Hulme said:

"You get the first hint of it in the beginnings of the Renaissance itself, in a person like Pico Della Mirandola. You get there the hint of an idea of something which finally culminates in a doctrine which is the opposite of the doctrine of Original Sin: the belief that man as a part of nature was after all something satisfactory. You get a change from a certain profundity and intensity to that flat and insipid optimism which, passing through its first stage of decay in Rousseau, has finally culminated in the state of slush in which we now have the misfortune to live."

The liking for Renaissance and post-Renaissance art comes through vitalism – an identification with nature, a taking pleasure in nature because we feel we are a part of nature. Abstract art on the contrary emphasises disjunction and separation from nature. Man is different. Man is moral and fundamentally religious. There is a part of man which transcends nature. Hulme said:

"We naturally do not call the geometrical arts *beautiful* because beauty is for us the satisfaction of a certain need, and that need is one which archaic art never set out to satisfy. What from our standpoint appears as the greatest distortion must have been, for the people who produced it, the highest beauty and the fulfilment of some other desire"

Hulme regarded Cezanne as one who in modern times was doing something very like what the archaic artists were doing, and he quotes his saying that nature could be reduced to,

"...the cone, the cylinder and the sphere."

The scope and depth of Hulme's thoughts were hugely influential on the whole movement that is broadly described as Modernism. C.H. Sisson wrote in his *English Poetry 1900–1950*:

"It is hardly too much to say that Hulme has been, in this country, one of the dominant minds of the century. He exposed humanism as the superstition of the Renaissance."

Hulme was extremely precocious, with a fertile mind ranging over anything of intellectual interest. Jones says:

"While still at school he thought he had discovered the differential calculus and was bitterly disappointed to find out that it had already been discovered by Newton and Leibnitz."

Although he was awarded an Exhibition in mathematics, Hulme seemed to regard any activity other than conversation as a waste of time and effort. He was academically lazy, rebellious and rowdy. He was physically tall and strong and preternaturally lively and exuberant. Patrick McGuinness said of him:

"Whether holding forth in his London rooms about Original Sin, enjoying riots in Paris or beating up Wyndham Lewis in a conflagration over a woman – Lewis ended up being suspended upside-down by his turn-ups from the railings of Great Ormond Street – Hulme is remembered as an energetic and irrepressible character."

He once persuaded Gaudier-Brzeska to make him a knuckle-duster carved out of solid brass and he afterwards carried this about with him wherever he went. Again Michael Roberts relates how:

"Once Hulme was making water in Soho Square in broad daylight when a policeman came up and said, *You can't do that here!* Hulme turned around and buttoned himself up and said, *Do you know you are addressing a member of the middle classes?* The policeman said, *I beg pardon, Sir,* and went on."

A.R. Jones again:

"Characteristic of the method adopted by Hulme in pursuing his amours was an occasion on which, sitting at a table in the Café Royal talking to his friends, Hulme suddenly looked at his watch and strode from the building with the remark, *I've a pressing engagement in five minutes' time.* In twenty minutes he had returned wiping his brow and complaining that the steel staircase of the emergency exit at Piccadilly Circus tube station was the most uncomfortable place in which he had ever copulated

"He more than once offered to marry Diana, Mrs Kibblewhite's young daughter when she grew up, because she made such fine treacle tart."

And he ate suet pudding nearly every day of his life while he lived in London. A sweet tooth and a taste for fornication, but a lifelong teetotaller, Hulme always professed himself a member of the Church of England. For Hulme, thought and belief were embodied in physical actions. Concretised emotionality. He understood that in order to *express,* we must *do.* And what we do may look irrational. For example he said:

"Such as pilgrimages to graves, standing bareheaded and similar freaks of a lover's fancy. The same can be observed in religion. A man cannot deliberately make up his mind to think of the goodness of God for an hour, but he can perform some ritual act of admiration whether it be the offering of a sacrifice or merely saying *Amen* to a set prayer. *By thine agony and bloody sweat*. By common effort, this phrase many times repeated gives an intensity of meaning. This intensity of meaning is what is sought for."

He said:

"I regard processions as the highest form of art. I cannot resist even the lowest form of them. I must march even with the Salvation Army bands I meet accidentally in Oxford Street on Sunday night."

Whether in Cambridge or Canada, where he worked as a labourer, he philosophised all the time, thoughts which found publication in his remarks collected as *Cinders*. The Canadian landscape affected him profoundly. As Jones says,

"In Canada he was haunted by the vast image of space, by the huge sky and the flat, rolling grasslands reaching out to the horizon. Like Pascal, he suffered the fright of the mind before the unknown."

We remember Pascal's saying about the terrifying infinite spaces.

On his return from Canada he taught English in Brussels for a while and learnt French and German. His combativeness never abated. For example, in 1908 he gave a lecture at The Poets' Club referring to the Club's President's views as,

"The kind of statement that I utterly detest."

He called for a new form of poetry based on close observation. There were a few others who thought like this and it was around this time that Hulme joined the group which included Flint and Pound who for a time were known as the Imagists. On the continent he was attracted to Charles Maurras and Action Francaise, notorious for its royalism, ultra-conservatism and anti-romanticism, its nationalism and respect for the church – but without necessarily believing in God. As Hulme's views developed, he began to criticise the sloppiness of romantic verse as but one symptom of the post-Rousseau attitude involving various aspects of rotten-ness: among which were democracy, progress, human perfectibility and the idea that man is innately good.

When war broke out, Hulme joined the Honourable Artillery Company and on 29th December 1914 he was sent to France. When he returned to England wounded the following year and In hospital, he took up the cudgels against pacifists (among them Bertrand Russell) with articles such as *The Kind of Rubbish We Oppose* and *Why We Are in Favour of This War* He wrote:

"The pacifists' incapacity to realise the consequences of defeat. It arises from a relativist, utilitarian ethic. They live securely and comfortably, finding a sufficient support in a sceptical rationalism. But individuals in a condition of danger, when the pseudo-absolutes melt away into a flux, require once more a real absolute to enable them to live."

The pacifism of Russell and Bell arose from a progressive utilitarian ideology that found no place whatever for the heroic, that deeply discounted the importance of honour and that was prepared to sacrifice virtually any principle for the sake of peace. Hulme had nothing but contempt for it:

"It comes to this: that for the emancipated man death is too great a price to pay for anything. Life and comfort are their ultimate goods."

Michael Roberts commented:

114

"Noting the socialist rhetoric with which the well-to-do Bell was wont to festoon his pacifist pretensions, Hulme made an observation that is as pertinent and withering today as it was in 1916: *It is a widespread but entirely mistaken idea to suppose that you amend for the advantages of wealth by asserting verbally that you are a socialist.*"

Roberts goes on to summarise Hulme's argument against the utilitarian pacifists:

"In the humanist view, everything is justified by its results, and the results are justified by *their* results and so on. The ultimate justification is either future happiness or human survival. This is totally opposed to the outlook that Hulme sometimes calls *religious* and sometimes *classical*. In that view, there are absolute goods, which are not justified by anything they may lead to, but are simply good in themselves. Restraint, courage, self-sacrifice and truthfulness are qualities of this kind. If people have no sense of the reality of these absolute values, they have no standard by which they can perceive the radical imperfection of either man or nature, and they begin to think that life is the source and measure of all values and that man is fundamentally good."

In the century since Hulme wrote, that *progressive* view has intensified and become so endemic that nowadays almost everyone is outraged to find it occasionally challenged. The century which has seen more suffering through wars and genocides than all the centuries together which preceded it, compliments itself on its intrinsic goodness and, even after Stalin, Hitler, Mao, Pol Pot, the atomic bomb, the death camps, the Balkan and the Rwandan massacres, declares itself innocent and, as it were, cries, *Nothing to acknowledge, nothing to bewail!*

Hulme believed that England ought to fight until Germany was beaten, because a German victory would have established German dominion from the North Sea to the Mediterranean. Recovering from his wounds, he mooched around London until March 1916 when he was commissioned into The Royal Marines Artillery. It was, as Michael Roberts says,

"On 28th September 1917, just when everybody seemed to have knocked off for lunch, there was an unexpected burst of shellfire and Hulme was killed."

Hulme's anti-vitalist, anti-Romantic view found expression in his political outlook and in 1912 he wrote a long article which he called *A Tory Philosophy*. He begins with characteristic gusto:

"It is my aim to explain in this article why I believe in Original Sin, why I can't stand Romanticism and why I am a certain kind of Tory. I am more than a conservative: I am a reactionary."

But here we must put far from our minds the vision of the modern Conservative Party and think instead of Dr Johnson and Samuel Coleridge, of T.S.Eliot and C.H. Sisson. Hulme developed a defence of classicism and royalism which we recognise later in Eliot's *Tradition and the Individual Talent* and his *Notes Towards the Definition of Culture* as well as in Sisson's *The Spirit of Public Administration* and his essay *Is There a Church of England?*
Hulme said:

"The classical attitude has a great respect for the past and for tradition not for sentimental but for purely rational grounds. Classicism does not believe in any real progress. The root of classicism is this, that if the rules are of no value without genius, yet there is in them more of genius than there is in any great genius himself. The idea of a personal inspiration jumping all complete from nature, capable of creating, by a kind of divine act, the whole organism of adaptable means of expression is ridiculous."

He defined the Romantic as someone

"...who is always just about to escape from something. Always escaping, that's it. The Romantic doesn't want to escape from anything in particular, but just that he shall escape. In politics this is associated with the idea of progress."

He declared that the engine of progress is the rise of science, and he scorned the arrogance of the scientists:

"Scientists seem to think that the discontinuities in nature are only apparent and that further investigation will reveal the underlying continuity."

Here our own thoughts might turn to Stephen Hawking and those other astrophysicists who confidently claim that we shall soon have, as Hawking promised in *A Brief History of Time*,

"...a Theory of Everything, and then we will know the mind of God."

But the complete answer to everything is always just around the corner, like the Red Queen's promise of *jam tomorrow*.

Against the accusation that he was bombastic, there is no defence except to say that he consistently gave reasons for his perpetual mood of vituperation, and he attempted to explain why traditionalists and conservatives had lost the culture wars against the Romantic and the progressive:

"We have been beaten because our enemies' theories have conquered us. We have played with those to our own undoing. Not until we are hardened again by conviction are we likely to do any good. In accepting the theories of the other side, we are merely repeating a well-known historical phenomenon. The Revolution in France came about not so much because the forces which should have resisted were half-hearted in their resistance. They themselves had been conquered intellectually by the theories of the revolutionary side. The privileged class is beaten only when it has lost faith in itself, when it has been penetrated by the ideas that are working against it."

And he asked,

"What is it which makes a man contemplate the idea of a constant world with such repugnance so that he insists, in spite of all evidence, that progress is continuous and that man may and does change? I am here getting at the sentiment which is the root of all the evil."

Precisely:

"The progressives and Romantics say there is no reason why we should not suppose that selfishness will be gradually eliminated and a new kind of man, better fitted to live in the Socialist Utopia, will be evolved. They don't believe in God, so they begin to believe that man is a god. They don't believe in heaven, so they begin to believe in a heaven on earth. In other words, you get Romanticism."

No one could ever accuse Hulme of being a systematic thinker, let alone an academic; and the closest he came to summarising his general outlook was in some remarks called *A Notebook* published in *The New Age* magazine in 1915 and 1916. He thought that scepticism, grown out of scientific materialism and mistaken ideas about human progress, is dangerous to the proper development of the mind:

"Living in a sceptical atmosphere you are in an unnatural attitude which prevents you seeing objective truth. For there is an absolute difference between men and animals. It is impossible to explain completely the nature of man as a complex development out of the animal world."

And in *A Notebook*, he identified and collected together the impediments to sound thinking:

"Romanticism in literature; Relativism in ethics; Idealism in philosophy; Modernism in religion."

And religion, for Hulme, is not simply the highest form of feeling: it is a different category altogether. But, as he says,

"Our difficulty now, of course, is that we are really incapable of understanding how any other view but the humanistic could be seriously held by intelligent and emancipated men."

In such luminous perceptions as that, he foresaw the triumph of the secular scientistic outlook which is our prevailing orthodoxy. People believe what they want to believe. For once, Hulme states this quite politely:

"Philosophers are moved by certain unconscious canons of satisfaction. The humanist canons are demonstrably false. The whole subject has been confused by the failure to recognise the gap between the regions of vital and human things and that of the absolute values of ethics and religion. We introduce into human things the perfection that properly belongs only to the divine, and thus confuse both human and divine things by not clearly separating them.

"The fundamental error is that of placing perfection in humanity, thus giving rise to that bastard thing *Personality* and all the bunkum that follows from it. You disguise the wheel by tilting it up a bit. It then becomes progress which is the modern substitute for religion."

He insisted,

"Ethical values are not relative to human desires and

feelings, but absolute and objective, and as man is essentially bad, he can only accomplish anything of value by discipline – ethical and political. Order is thus not merely negative but creative and liberating. Institutions are necessary. Moreover, the Medieval period regarded Christian doctrines as *facts*. These beliefs were the centre of their whole civilisation and even the character of their economic life was regulated by them.

"And at the beginning of the Christian period you have many of the Fathers continuing the classical conception of man. At the same time as St Augustine, you get Pelagius who has many resemblances to Rousseau and might easily be applauded at a meeting of progressives."

The most incisive comments Hulme makes on the modern attitude of progressivism and human perfectibility are where he says:

"The best-known work on the Renaissance, while valuable historically, seems to me to miss the whole point, for this reason: it describes the emergence of a new attitude towards life, of the new conception of man, as it might describe the gradual discovery of the concept of gravitation – that is, as the gradual emergence of something which once established would remain always, the period before it being characterised as a privation of the new thing. The whole point of the thing is missed if we do not recognise that the new attitude towards man at the Renaissance was thus just an *attitude*, one attitude among other possible ones, deliberately chosen. It is better to describe it as a heresy, a mistaken adoption of false conceptions.

"The moderns, whether philosophers or reformers, make constant appeals to certain ideals which they assume everybody will admit as natural and inevitable for the emancipated man. What these are you may discover from perorations of speeches – even from scrapbooks, *To thine own true self etc...* Over the portal of the new world *Be thyself* shall be written. Culture is not satisfied till we all come to a perfect man...the free growth of personality and so on. We think these things not because they are inevitable ways of thinking but because we absorb them unconsciously from the humanist tradition which moulds the actual apparatus of our thought. They can all be traced back to the Stoics, Epicureans and pantheists of the Renaissance. The detailed exposition of the process by which this attitude was gradually embodied in the conceptual apparatus we inherit may do more than anything else to convince us how very far it is from being an inevitable attitude.

"The pseudo-categories of the humanist attitude are thought to be on the same footing as the objective categories of space and time. It is thought to be impossible for an emancipated man to think sincerely in the categories of the religious attitude."

In two lucid paragraphs, A.R. Jones extracts what Hulme meant by the religious attitude:

"To aim towards perfection, whether in knowledge, speech or action, is right; but to expect to be rewarded by attainment is to misunderstand the whole nature of human life and activity. It is this error that leads to disillusion, and the disillusion has nothing to do with the decay of a race and the death of its gods. It is a stage on the way to health; and we can pass beyond it to a new certainty and confidence.

"There is nothing gloomy or pessimistic in the tragic view of life. The tragic view recognises from the beginning all those facts that lead to disappointment and bitterness and therefore it leaves room for a gaiety that is not at the mercy of circumstances. The tragic view is neces-

sary because the Romanticism of Victor Hugo, the sentimental optimism of liberal pacifists and the utopian faith
in automatic progress are untenable. Many people who
had placed their hope in these things find themselves
reduced to a despair that would be pitiful if it were not
silly. In the history of every civilisation a time comes when
the race loses its confidence in its gods, its values and its
mission; and then, in some way not understood, it begins
to die out and less civilised races take its place. In Western
Europe today, there is a decline in courage, faith and hope
that seems exactly like the decline that led to the fall of
Athens, Sparta and Rome."

Hulme concludes *A Notebook* with this mighty peroration:

"I want to emphasise as clearly as I can that I attach very
little value indeed to the *sentiments* attaching to the religious attitude. I hold quite coldly and intellectually, as it
were, that the way of thinking about the world and man,
the conception of sin and the categories which ultimately
make up the religious attitude, are the true categories
and the right way of thinking.

"I have none of the feelings of nostalgia, the reverence
for tradition, the desire to recapture the sentiment of
Fra Angelico, which seems to animate most modern
defenders of religion. All that seems to me to be bosh.
What is important is what nobody seems to realise – the
dogmas like that of Original Sin, which are the closest
expression of the categories of the religious attitude. That
man is in no sense perfect, but a wretched creature who
can yet apprehend perfection. It is not then that I might
put up with the dogma for the sake of the sentiment, but
that I may possibly swallow the sentiment for the sake of
the dogma. Very few since the Renaissance have really
understood the dogma, certainly very few inside the
churches in recent years. If they appear occasionally even
fanatical about the very world of the dogma, that is only

a secondary result of belief really grounded in sentiment. Certainly no humanist could understand the dogma. They all chatter about matters which are, in comparison with this, quite secondary notions – God, Freedom and Immortality."

But we should end as we began with his poems – which Eliot described as,

"Some of the most beautiful short poems in the English language":

Sunset II

"I love not the Sunset
That flaunts like a scarlet sore
O'er a half sick sky,
That calls aloud for all to gape
At its beauty
Like a wanton.

"But Sunset when the sun comes home
Like a ship from the sea
With its round red sail
Shadowed against a clear sky,
Silent, in a cool harbour
At eve,
After labour."

This is the antidote to all Romantic waffle about *nature*. It is the purifying language of the hard, true image. Some of these poems are so short as to be just singular evocations, snapshots of reality"

"Old houses were scaffolding once
And workmen whistling."

And

"The lark crawls on the cloud
Like a flea on a white body."

"The world lives in order to develop lines on its face."
"The mystic sadness of the sight
Of a far town seen in the night."

"The flounced edge of a skirt
Recoiling like waves off a cliff."

"Down the long desolate street of stars."

How close was Hulme to becoming a practising Christian?
A.R. Jones says:

"Reason is not complete unless it includes humility; and humility involves the recognition of tradition and authority. It is difficult to see how for a Western European the authority could be any other than the Christian Church. Soon after Hulme's death, one of his closet friends, Ramiro de Maeztu, wrote: *I believe that in essentials he was already a Catholic, although not in the ritual sense but in the spiritual.*"

Long after Hulme's death Ezra Pound said,

"The black and smeary 1920s wretchedly needed his guidance and the pity is that he wasn't there to keep down the vermin. God knows Mr Lewis and Mr Eliot must have had a lonely time."

Chapter Six

T.S. Eliot (1888–1965)

Thomas Stearns Eliot was born in St Louis and educated at Harvard. After a year in Paris, he returned to Harvard and studied philosophy under George Santayana and Bertrand Russell. On a travelling scholarship he spent a year at Merton College, Oxford and began a doctoral thesis on F.H. Bradley. In 1911 he met Ezra Pound who admired his poetry and encouraged him to stay in England.

After a year as a schoolmaster at Highgate, where he taught John Betjeman, and High Wycombe, he joined the foreign exchange department at Lloyds Bank in the City of London where he worked for eight years before becoming a director of Faber's. He published *Prufrock and Other Observations* in 1917 and *The Waste Land* in 1922. *The Hollow Men* followed in 1925. He edited the influential political and literary magazine *The Criterion* from 1923–1939.

In 1927 Eliot became a naturalised British subject and was baptised into the Church of England. His volume of essays *For Lancelot Andrewes* (1928) identified him as an Anglo Catholic. He published the poem *Ash Wednesday* in 1930 and the dramas *The Rock* (1934) and *Murder in the Cathedral* (1935). These were followed by four plays which were successful in the West End but which, steeped as they were in classical and Christian references, bewildered the critics. Many regard *Four Quartets* (1936–1942) as the finest of his long poems. Eliot was a churchwarden of his parish church, Saint Stephen's, Gloucester Road, London, and a life member of the Society of King Charles the Martyr.

Eliot combined the gifts of poet, playwright and critic. His outstanding works of literary criticism included *The Sacred Wood* (1920) and *The Use of Poetry and the Use of Criticism*

(1933). He also wrote *The Idea of a Christian Society* (1939) and *Notes Towards the Definition of Culture* (1948).

In 1915 he married Vivienne Haigh-Wood. The marriage was not successful and the couple separated. Many years later Eliot wrote,

> "I came to persuade myself that I was in love with Vivienne simply because I wanted to burn my boats and commit myself to staying in England. And she persuaded herself (under the influence of Pound) that she would save the poet by keeping him in England. To her, the marriage brought no happiness. To me, it brought the state of mind out of which came *The Waste Land.*"

After Vivienne's death, Eliot married, in 1957, Valerie Fletcher. In 1948 he was awarded the Nobel Prize for Literature and was admitted to the Order of Merit by King George VI.

As former Rector of St Michael's, Cornhill, I have some slight connection with Eliot for the branch of Lloyds where he worked was in my parish. A few years ago I met an old man whose father had known Eliot in those days. He recalled how the poet would often stand with his arms outstretched outside the doors of the bank and recite two lines from *The Waste Land:*

> "To where St Mary Woolnoth kept the hours
> With a dead sound on the final stroke of nine."

Only then would he enter the office and begin the day's work. Like the James brothers – not Jesse and Frank, but Henry and William – before him, he was a devotee of the old European culture. He wove his poems out of the stuff of Greek myths and drama; Dante, the metaphysical poets and the Anglican divines of the 17th century – Lancelot Andrewes in particular. In fact, *The Journey of the Magi* is part-lifted word for word from one of Andrewes' sermons. When confronted with this theft, Eliot said,

"The bad poet borrows; the good poet steals."

Eliot's long spiritual journey led him from the bleakness and dryness of *The Waste Land* to the temper which, by the time he came to write *Four Quartets*, he summed up as:

"Anglicanism, Royalism and Classicalism."

It might be said that a great part of Eliot's vocation was to teach the English their own traditional culture. Anthony Burgess wrote:

"When the news of Eliot's death came through, commercial television had just presented an abridgement of Middleton's *The Changeling*. Watching it, I thought that this could never have happened if Eliot hadn't opened our eyes to the greatness of the Jacobeans. Spike Milligan on a comic TV show could say, *Not with a banger but a Wimpy*, and most of the audience caught the reference. Weather forecasters joke about April being *the cruellest month*. Demagogues would quote John Donne and make titles out of Donne's poems or religious meditations. The metaphysical poets, still quaint and unreadable in my schooldays, became A-level set books. And, though not everybody could follow Eliot to the final austerities of Anglicanism, Royalism and Classicalism, his affirmation of the importance of tradition was accepted by the *avant garde.* For, with Eliot, the past was not a dull and venerable ancestor, but a living force which modified the present and was in turn modified by it. Time was not an army of unalterable law: time was a kind of ectoplasm."

This was Eliot's achievement: to take the old and, in Ezra Pound's phrase,

"Make it new".

As Eliot himself wrote, his aim was:

"To purify the dialect of the tribe."

The tribe was, of course, the English tribe. And Eliot sought to do this work of purification by penetrating to the centre of the classical style and reworking it in his own version of modern English:

"Unreal City,
Under the brown fog of a winter dawn,
A crowd flowed over London Bridge, so many,
I had not though death had undone so many."

It is Dante's *Inferno* rewritten by the poet on his way to the bank. Eliot was convinced that our neglect of the classics, our desertion of the church and our growing affection for international committees would lead inexorably to the decline of the nation. His prophetic words were mostly written between 1922 and 1942, and of course every prophet speaks first not to the future but to his contemporaries. But it would be a rash person who said that these words have lost their application today:

"I journeyed to London, to the time-kept City,
Where the river flows with foreign flotations.
There I was told: we have too many churches
And too few chop houses. There I was told:
Let the vicars retire. Men do not need the church
In the place where they work, but where they spend their
Sundays.
In the City we need no bells:
Let them waken the suburbs.
I journeyed to the suburbs, and there I was told:
We toil for six days, on the seventh we must motor
To Hindhead or Maidenhead.
In industrial districts, there I was told
Of economic laws.
In the pleasant countryside, there it seemed
That the country now is only fit for picnics,

And the church does not seem to be wanted
In country or in suburb; and in the town
Only for important weddings."

Thirty years before the reductionist, demythologising theologians of the 1960s rejoiced that humankind had now
come of age and had no use for traditional religion, Eliot
correctly saw that the attempt to build a secular morality
and to regard supernatural religion as something we have
outgrown would lead to social collapse:

"Do you need to be told that even such modest attainments
As you can boast in the way of polite society
Will hardly survive the Faith to which they owe their
significance?"

It is the same point made recently by Professor Marcello
Pera, former President of the Italian Senate:

"Christianity is so consubstantial with the West that any
surrender on its part would have devastating consequences. But will the Church, the clergy and the faithful,
be able to and want to be purified of the relativism that
has almost erased their identity and weakened their
message and witness?"

Eliot understood the profound disturbance in modern
society which was coming about through the progressive
disowning of its Christian roots:

"The whole of modern literature is corrupted by what I
call Secularism, that is simply unaware of, simply cannot
understand the meaning of, the primacy of the supernatural over the natural life: of something which I assume to
be our primary concern."

Moreover, he percipiently located this shift in the focus

of modern writing to the rise of the 19ᵗʰ century agnostic liberals who regarded poetry as an adequate replacement for the faith they had abandoned:

> "Matthew Arnold was too temperate and reasonable a man to maintain exactly that religious instruction is best conveyed by poetry, and he himself had very little to convey; but he discovered a new formula: poetry is not religion, but it is a capital substitute for religion – not invalid port, which may lead to hypocrisy, but coffee without caffeine and tea without tannin. To ask of poetry that it give religious and philosophical satisfaction, while deprecating philosophy and dogmatic religion, is of course to embrace the shadow of a shade. *Literature and Dogma* seems to me a valiant attempt to mediate between Newman and Huxley, but Arnold's mind was unsuited and ill-equipped: in philosophy and theology he was an undergraduate; in religion a Philistine."

In *Choruses from the Rock*, Eliot foresaw our misplaced trust in secular systems, committees, and initiatives, as we imagine that, if only we can get the socio-political processes right, we shall have an end to our society's problems. He says that the church tells us:

> "...of Evil and Sin, and other unpleasant facts.
> They constantly try to escape
> From the darkness outside and within
> By dreaming of systems so perfect that no one will need to be good."

Dreaming of systems so perfect... Is there a better definition of political correctness than that?

A government which thinks we can abolish mass murder by blaming hand guns rather than punishing the hands of those who fire them would do well to remember those lines. In fact we have recently learnt what was entirely predictable – that crimes involving hand guns have increased by thirty per cent since they were banned. Or think of the United Nations and the modern world of so called *peacekeeping* by international committee and then read these words:

"A commission is appointed
To confer with a Volscian commission
About perpetual peace...
What shall I cry?
We demand a committee
a representative committee
a committee of investigation
RESIGN RESIGN RESIGN."

He made a similar point in prose on the eve of the Second World War:

"The current terms in which we discuss international affairs and political theory may only tend to conceal from us the real issues of contemporary civilisation."

And for those who see the ideal politics in the paradoxical policies of, on the one hand, devolving and so emasculating the United Kingdom and, on the other, surrendering national sovereignty to European Union, he had this to say:

"A decentralisation under central direction is a contradiction."

The General Synod of the Church of England and the bureaucracy of its Board for Social Responsibility – which has a policy on everything from glue sniffing to global warming – acts as if it believes that the more paperwork it tosses in the direction of the parish clergy, the sooner all our social problems will be relieved. The Synod might come to see its own state of mind described in these words:

"Distracted from distraction by distraction
Filled with fancies and empty of meaning

Tumid apathy with no concentration,
Men and bits of paper."

The cult of the mass media was in its infancy in the 1930s when people regarded advertisements as quite charming and cute novelties, but Eliot could see already what it would become if allowed to develop unchecked:

"The increasing organisation of advertisement and prop-aganda – or the influencing of masses of men by any means except through their intelligence – is all against them."

Eliot did not live to see the deterioration in the conduct of political affairs and in all our institutions by which every aspect of public life has the appearance of an advertise-ment, while national and local elections are organised as if they were part of the entertainments industry. Again he speaks of the policy of:

"...destroying traditional social habits of the people by licensing the opinions of the most foolish."

One wonders what words Eliot would have had left to comment on our focus groups, the empty-headed celebrity culture and the voyeuristic unreality of oxymoronic *reality television.* Eliot might have been speaking to the drivel and chatter about the sex lives of pop stars and the health fads with which even the broadsheet newspapers are now filled. And when it comes to *destroying traditional social habits*, we might consider the results of the ban on foxhunting, seven days a week shopping, the twenty-four hours a day cities and Internet browsing that have all but abolished sleep.

Eliot saw that the coming of mass entertainment would lead to lives being lived as if life itself were only a form of distraction and that the consequences would be the same as those which followed the dereliction of the *bread and circuses* which characterised the decline of the Roman

132

Empire. No doubt he had in his mind the desert fathers and the small groups of Christians who took themselves off into the countryside and formed the beginning of the monastic movement when he wrote:

"For this immediate future, perhaps for a long way ahead, the continuity of culture may have to be maintained by a very small number of people indeed – and these not necessarily equipped with worldly advantages. It will not be the large organs of opinion or the old periodicals; it must be the small and obscure papers and reviews, those which are hardly read by anyone but their own contributors, that will keep critical thought alive and encourage authors of original talent. I wish that a periodical could be sold like admission to a theatre, at a varying scale of prices..."

At the same time he said also:

"The tendency of unlimited industrialism is to create bodies of men and women of all classes detached from tradition, alienated from religion and susceptible to mass suggestion: in other words, a mob. And a mob will be no less a mob if it is well-fed, well clothed and well-housed."

Many would today see exactly this well-fed mob in the consumer-welfare society, with its binge-drinking underclass rampant and out of control, in which *the poor* spend a hundred pounds on designer trainers, even more on the latest football strip and a fortune on mindless computer games. For a people to survive they have to fill their lives with things other than diversions and entertainments. Eliot understood this:

"The psychologist W.H.R. Rivers adduced evidence which has led him to believe that the natives of Melanesia are dying out principally for the reason that the *civilisation* forced upon them has deprived them of all interest in life. They are dying from pure boredom. When every theatre has been replaced by a hundred cinemas, when every musical instrument has been replaced by a hundred gramophones, when every horse has been replaced by a hundred cheap motor-cars, when electrical ingenuity has made it possible for every child to hear its bedtime stories from a loudspeaker, when applied science has done everything possible with the materials on this earth to make life as interesting as possible, it will be surprising if the population of the entire civilised world does not rapidly follow the fate of the Melanesians."

He saw the coming redefinition of *poverty* as early as 1948 when he said:

"The term social justice is in danger of losing its rational context."

When we hear rock music on even the so called *serious* networks and find it featured at the Promenade Concerts, when we see the names of drug-addicted pop stars appearing in the Honours Lists and when a work of art is defined as *anything anyone wants to say it is*, we discover again Eliot the prophet in these words:

"A mass culture will always be a substitute culture: and sooner or later the deception will become apparent to the more intelligent of those upon whom the mass culture has been palmed off."

He added:

"The culture of a people is the incarnation of its religion."

It makes us pause to wonder what perversion of religion we are seeing reflected in contemporary mass culture. Commenting on Eliot's words, Professor Stephen Clark has given us the up-to-date, *non-judgemental, non-discrimi-*

natory view of our contemporary secular religion and its watchword *diversity*:

"Unregulated hedonism easily concludes that any pleasurable contact of two skins is as good as any other. Radical amoralism judges that anything can be the object and occasion of a sexual desire. None are more natural than another."

A society which has abandoned its capacity to judge and for which discrimination is now only a word of disapprobation, has lost its mind and, as a consequence, its morality and its soul. We are frequently told that the remedy for the decline of public life is *Education, Education, Education*. But what sort of education? Eliot long ago had an accurate vision of the horrors to come:

"We are told now that the highest achievements of the past in art, in wisdom, in holiness were but *stages in development* which we can teach our youngsters to improve upon. We are told we must not impose traditional culture upon the young, though we may impose upon them whatever political and social philosophy is in vogue. There is no doubt that in our headlong rush to educate everyone we are lowering standards, destroying our ancient edifices to make ready the ground upon which the barbarian hordes will encamp in their mechanised caravans."

Eliot's own view of what constitutes education was, as usual, stated briskly:

"Thought, study, mortification, sacrifice: it is such notions as these that should be impressed upon the young."

Eliot the great poet was at one with Eliot the great critic and so he emphasised this truth in verse:

"...the past has another pattern
and ceases to be a mere sequence –

Or even development: the latter a partial fallacy
Encouraged by superficial notions of evolution,
Which becomes, in the popular mind, a means of
disowning the past."

Moreover, and closely related to those popular ideas about evolution, we find the burgeoning dogma of *progress*. But,

"We do not assume that there is progress in art."

Eliot asked where we should look now for higher learning when the idea of the university has been so comprehensively debased?

"The universities of Europe should have their common ideals. They should have their obligations towards each other. They should be independent of the governments of the countries in which they are situated. They should not be institutions for the training of an efficient bureaucracy, or for equipping scientists to get the better of foreign scientists. They should stand for the preservation of learning, for the pursuit of truth, and, in so far as men are capable of it, the attainment of wisdom."

If the universities were failing in Eliot's day, they are nothing short of disastrous today, having taken into themselves things that are alien and poisonous to their existence: *tourism and media studies* to give just two examples of the falling off that there has been. Not that there is anything wrong with tourism and media studies, but the university is not the place for them: the university, as Eliot insisted, must be a place where excellence is cultivated and learning is pursued for its own sake. Universities are not meant to be utilitarian institutions. They are not *for* anything or *in order that.* The cultivation of excellence in the pursuit of understanding and knowledge is an end in itself. Would those who deprecate elitism suggest we pursue mediocrity instead?

The health and strength of our civilisation and the cure for our woes, said Eliot, is to understand the nature of our cultural history and so to imbibe it, that it becomes the motivating part of us. This is a living process and an active vocation and it is not:

"...to ring the bell backward
Nor is it an incantation
To summon the spectre of a rose
...or follow an antique drum."

Is all this looking back to the great writers of the past really necessary? All these arcane references and recondite quotations, are they not just part of what Philip Larkin disparaged as *the myth kitty which we can do without*? Eliot replied as follows:

"Someone said, *The dead writers are remote from us because we know so much more than they did.* Precisely, and they are that which we know."

Tradition is not a fossilised thing or part of the heritage industry: it is the constant renewal of our culture by innovations which are created out of a past that has been digested, a history that is understood. As we have seen, and as Marcello Pera along with many others remarked, western culture was formed to a very large extent out of Christianity and it will not survive the neglect of the faith. The enemy of a living religious culture is the utilitarian principle which in our day has degenerated into a valueless consumerism in which even the tenets of Christianity are invoked to support the technological-Benthamite suppositions of a decayed society. We have a destructive habit of getting hold of the wrong end of the stick, for, says Eliot:

"To justify Christianity because it provides a foundation for morality, instead of showing the necessity of Christian morality from the truth of Christian doctrine is a very dangerous inversion... It is not enthusiasm but dogma that differentiates a Christian from a pagan society."

And he indicated another common inversion:

"The persons who enjoy the biblical writings solely because of their literary merit are essentially parasites; and we know that parasites, when they become too numerous, are pests. I could fulminate against the men of letters who have gone into ecstasies over *the Bible as literature, the Bible as the noblest monument of English prose.* Those who talk of the Bible as *a monument of English prose* are merely admiring it as a monument over the grave of Christianity."

But Eliot did not wish to see a Christian State: he acknowledged a place in the good society for adherents of other faiths and even freethinkers. But he warned of the dire consequences which must follow if we deny the history that has made us what we are. The attempt to abolish or rewrite the past and to begin civilisation all over again, as it were from year zero, as first the French revolutionists and then the Soviets tried to do, will always result in a murderous regime and the reign of terror. Eliot spelt it out:

"An individual European may not even believe that the Christian Faith is true, but what he says and makes and does will all spring out of this history of European culture and depend upon that culture for its meaning. Only a Christian culture could have produced a Nietzsche or a Voltaire. I do not believe that the culture of Europe could survive the complete disappearance of the Christian Faith. And I am convinced of that not merely because I am a Christian myself, but as a student of social biology. If Christianity goes, the whole of our culture goes. Then you must start painfully again, and you cannot put on a new culture ready-made. You must wait for the grass to grow to feed the sheep to give the wool out of which your new coat will be made. You must pass through many centuries of barbarism. We should not live to see the new culture, nor would our great-great-great grandchildren: and if we did, not one of us would be happy in it."

It might be asked, if Christian civilisation is supposed to have been in the wrong all these centuries, on the basis of what is it supposed we can put it right? Even recent unbelief has its roots in faith: Nietzsche could only say that God is dead because Moses had first said that God is alive. It is spiritual truth alone that can repair us and this requires, as well as intelligence, reflective contemplation on the whole history of what has made us what we are. And where better to begin this than in church, but not as a blundering tourist:

"...you are not here to verify,
Instruct yourself, or inform curiosity
Or carry report. You are here to kneel
Where prayer has been valid. And prayer is more
Than an order of words, the conscious occupation
Of the praying mind, or the sound of the voice praying.
And what the dead had no speech for, when living,
They can tell you, being dead: the communication
Of the dead is tongued with fire beyond the language of
the living."

And specifically,

"We need to rediscover the sense of religious fear, so that it may be overcome by religious hope."

There is a divine purpose in human life and it has its appointed end:

"We shall not cease from exploration
And the end of all our exploring
Will be to arrive where we started
And know the place for the first time.

Through the unknown, remembered gate
When the last of earth left to discover
Is that which was the beginning;
At the source of the longest river
The voice of the hidden waterfall
And the children in the apple tree
Not known, because not looked for
But heard, half-heard, in the stillness
Between two waves of the sea.
Quick, now, here, now, always –
A condition of complete simplicity
(Costing not less than everything)
And all shall be well and
All manner of thing shall be well
When the tongues of flame are in-folded
Into the crowned knot of fire
And the fire and the rose are one."

Eliot has a partially unjustified reputation for obscurity, and his poetry has been described as arcane. Some of it does demand a big effort, but there is a reason for this. Eliot regards all great writers as our contemporaries and all great literature as contributing to human understanding and wisdom. Therefore, he does not wish us to read only, say, *The Waste Land* but to follow up the connections he makes in that poem with such as Dante, the Old Testament, Shakespeare, the Jacobean playwrights and the ancient Greeks. He hopes that we will be prepared to do this work because he believes that the reward will more than repay the labour. Parts of *The Waste Land* are obscure, and so perhaps is *Ash Wednesday* and some of the shorter and more experimental poems. But hundreds of lines in Eliot are spectacularly lucid and of great beauty. There is also much humour. There is mimicry. There is fervent prophecy, the meaning of which is never in doubt. There is wonderful evocation:

For example, is there a picture of autumn in the City more effective than the following:

"The yellow fog that rubs its back upon the window-
panes,
The yellow smoke that rubs its muzzle on the window-
panes,
Licked its tongue into the corners of the evening,
Lingered upon the pools that stand in drains,
Let fall upon its back the soot that falls from chimneys,
Slipped by the terrace, made a sudden leap,
And seeing that it was a soft October night,
Curled once about the house and fell asleep."

Spiritualism and divination by the Tarot were highly fashionable among the dining classes in the early years of the 20th
century. Eliot wittily satirises the fortune-telling session:

"Madame Sosostris, famous clairvoyante,
Had a bad cold, nevertheless
Is known to be the wisest woman in Europe,
With a wicked pack of cards. Here, said she,
Is your card, the drowned Phoenician Sailor,
(Those are pearls that were his eyes) Look!
Here is Belladonna, the Lady of the Rocks,
The lady of situations.
Here is the man with three staves, and here is the Wheel,
And here is the one-eyed merchant, and this card,
Which is blank, is something he carries on his back,
Which I am forbidden to see. I do not find
The Hanged Man. Fear death by water.
I see crowds of people, walking round in a ring.
Thank you. If you see dear Mrs Equitone,
Tell her I bring the horoscope myself:
One must be so careful these days."

The East End pub scene which follows the fortune telling
session was much copied by Harold Pinter and the kitchen
sink dramatists of the 1950s. We are a long way from the
elitist, classicist, royalist Anglicanism here:

"When Lil's husband got demobbed, I said –
I didn't mince my words, I said to her myself,
HURRY UP PLEASE ITS TIME
Now Albert's coming back, make yourself a bit smart.
He'll want to know what you done with that money he gave you
To get yourself some teeth. He did, I was there,
You have them all out, Lil, and get a nice set,
He said, I swear, I can't bear to look at you….

….HURRY UP PLEASE ITS TIME
Goonight Bill. Goonight Lou. Goonight May. Goonight.
Ta ta. Goonight. Goonight.
Good night ladies, good night, sweet ladies, good night,
good night."

He is capable of showing profound melancholy, loneliness
and despair as in, for instance, the accurately wrought lines
about the typist taken advantage of by her insensitive,
unwanted lover:

"The typist home at teatime, clears her breakfast, lights
Her stove, and lays out food in tins.
Out of the window perilously spread
Her drying combinations touched by the sun's last rays,
On the divan are piled (at night her bed)
Stockings, slippers, camisoles and stays.
I Tiresias, old man with wrinkled dugs
Perceived the scene, and foretold the rest –
I too awaited the expected guest.
He, the young man carbuncular, arrives,
A small house-agent's clerk, with one bold stare,
One of the low on whom assurance sits
As a silk hat on a Bradford millionaire.
The time is now propitious, as he guesses,
The meal is ended, she is bored and tired,
Endeavours to engage her in caresses
Which still are unreproved, if undesired.

Flushed and decided, he assaults at once;
Exploring hands encounter no defence;
His vanity requires no response,
And makes a welcome of indifference.
(And I Tiresias have foresuffered all
Enacted on this same divan or bed;
I who have sat by Thebes below the wall
And walked among the lowest of the dead)
Bestows one final patronising kiss,
And gropes his way, finding the stairs unlit...
She turns and looks a moment in the glass,
Hardly aware of her departed lover;
Her brain allows one half-formed thought to pass:
'Well now that's done: and I'm glad it's over.'
When lovely woman stoops to folly and
Paces about her room again, alone,
She smooths her hair with automatic hand,
And puts a record on the gramophone."

Good for us if we catch the reference to Oliver Goldsmith, and better still if we feel the weight of Tiresias' world-weary sadness at human sin and folly which persists in the London bedsit in 1922 just as it did in ancient Thebes. But we do not need to spot either of these connections to weep for the sadness of the young woman, misused and deserted. And how Eliot captures and delineates the gestures and demeanour of both the slobbering lecher and his melancholy victim!

In the matter of prophecy, too, the poet – unlike his creation the fraudulent medium, Madame Sosostris – leaves us in no doubt as to the import of his message:

"The endless cycle of idea and action,
Endless invention, endless experiment,
Brings knowledge of motion, but not of stillness;
Knowledge of speech, but not of silence;
Knowledge of words, and ignorance of the Word.
All our knowledge brings us nearer to our ignorance,

All our ignorance brings us nearer to death,
But nearness to death no nearer to God.
Where is the Life we have lost in living?
Where is the wisdom we have lost in knowledge?
Where is the knowledge we have lost in information?
The cycles of heaven in twenty centuries
Bring us farther from God and nearer to the Dust."

That is as true a picture of *ennui* in the contemporary world of information technology and the worldwide web as we could hope for. His range is wider than most poets and, when he so wished, Eliot could write with all the luminous, tactile, aromatic nuance of the nature poet:

"Time and the bell have buried the day,
The black cloud carries the sun away.
Will the sunflower turn to us, will the clematis
Stray down, bend to us; tendril and spray
Clutch and cling?
Chill
Fingers of yew be curled
Down on us? After the kingfisher's wing
Has answered light to light, and is silent, the light is still
At the still point of the turning world."

He could write an elegy, a valediction, supremely capturing that mixture of nostalgia, regret, self-loathing and disappointment which so often accompanies old age:

"It was not (to start again) what one had expected.
What was to be the value of the long looked forward to,
Long hoped for calm, the autumnal serenity
And the wisdom of age? Had they deceived us,
Or deceived themselves, the quiet-voiced elders,
Bequeathing us merely a receipt for deceit?"

In a most affecting passage, which we read without the slightest difficulty, he proclaims the wisdom of the only

144

self-knowledge worth striving for: that which leads to penitence and charity:

> "Let me disclose the gifts reserved for age
> To set a crown upon your lifetime's effort.
> First, the cold friction of expiring sense
> Without enchantment, offering no promise
> But bitter tastelessness of shadow fruit
> As body and soul begin to fall asunder.
> Second, the conscious impotence of rage
> At human folly, and the laceration
> Of laughter at what ceases to amuse.
> At last, the rending pain of re-enactment
> Of all that you have done, and been; the shame
> Of motives late revealed, and the awareness
> Of things ill done and done to others' harm
> That once you took for exercise of virtue."

There is a strong case for naming Eliot as both the best poet and the best critic of the 20th century. And the cure for imagining him to be difficult is the same as that which Ezra Pound proposed at Possum's funeral:

> "Read him!"

Chapter Seven

R.G. Collingwood (1889–1943)

R.G. Collingwood was born in Cartmel in Lancashire. His father, W.G. Collingwood, was an archaeologist, painter, and sometime private secretary to John Ruskin. His mother was also a painter and a more than competent pianist. Collingwood was taught at home by his father until, when he was thirteen, he was sent to prep school and a year later to Rugby. In 1908 he went to University College, Oxford, to read *Literae Humaniores*. He so impressed his teachers that he was accorded the rare distinction of being made a Fellow (of Pembroke) even before his final examinations in 1912.

He turned to philosophy and was much influenced by the realists E.F. Carritt and John Cook Wilson. Gradually he came to reject the realist view as a result of his reading of Benedetto Croce, Giovanni Gentile and especially through his friendship with J.A. Smith, Waynflete Professor of Metaphysical Philosophy from 1910 to 1935. In 1913 he translated Croce's *The Philosophy of Giambattista Vico*. Collingwood's first book was *Religion and Philosophy* (1916).

While still a fellow of Pembroke, he took up archaeological work and spent his summers supervising excavations of Roman sites in the north of England. He became an authority on Roman Britain through his hundreds of published papers. His books on the subject, especially his work on Roman inscriptions, are still highly regarded almost a century after their publication.

Collingwood's most important philosophical books are *An Essay on Philosophical Method* (1933) and *An Essay on Metaphysics* (1940). He was always a great synthesist as he demonstrated in *Speculum Mentis (1924)*. This was a synopsis of the various forms of experience: art, religion, science, history and philosophy. He also lectured on moral philosophy, Roman history, the principles of historical study and aesthetics. He published *The Principles of Art* in 1937, the year after his *Roman Britain and The English Settlements.*

He set himself a relentlessly punishing schedule of work and his health began to deteriorate seriously from the early 1930s. Suffering from high blood pressure, he was given leave of absence from the university. Upon his return towards the end of 1932, he started to write what was to become one of his finest achievements in philosophy *An Essay on Philosophical Method*, published in 1933. Concurrently he worked and lectured on the philosophy of history and the philosophy of nature, though his important books on these subjects were published only posthumously: *The Idea of Nature* (1945) and *The Idea of History* (1946).

In 1935 Collingwood was appointed Waynflete Professor of Metaphysical Philosophy and moved to Magdalen. He had already been elected a Fellow of the British Academy in 1934. While seeing *The Principles of Art* through the press, he suffered the first of many strokes and feared that he would not live to complete all the work he had set himself across the whole field of philosophy, history, art criticism and ethics. He used a convalescent voyage to the East Indies to write his *Autobiography* (1939). As what he called his *war effort* he published *The New Leviathan*, subtitled *Man, Society, Civilisation and Barbarism.*

Collingwood died in Coniston in January 1943, aged only 53. He was buried in the churchyard there, between his parents and John Ruskin.

One might reasonably expect that the titles a writer chooses for his books would indicate their contents and to a degree this is true of Collingwood's books, but *only* to a degree. He is remarkable because he is profound, profuse and diverse. So we find a brilliant piece of analysis of, say, a particular political development in a book which, from its title, purports to be about painting. For example, in *The Principles of Art*, we find this:

"From Plato onwards, Greco-Roman society was living its life as a rearguard action against emotional bankruptcy. The critical moment was reached when Rome created an urban proletariat whose only function was to eat free bread and watch free shows. This meant the segregation of an entire class which had no work to do whatever; no positive function in society, whether economic or military or administrative or intellectual or religious; only the business of being supported and amused. When that had been done, it was only a question of time until Plato's nightmare of a consumer society came true: the drones set up their own king, and the story of the hive came to an end."

Collingwood was no mere *specialist* in the derogatory sense in which the word has come to describe a person whose life's work can be seen as progressively coming to know more and more about less and less. Astonished, we see that Collingwood was a specialist on just about every subject under the sun. Indeed, he does not recognise the activity of classifying knowledge according to various areas of study and discipline. He simply regards knowledge as knowledge and proceeds to follow the line of enquiry wherever it may lead, frequently turning sharply aside along some unbeaten track or, as it were, down a road which appears to be leading somewhere entirely different from where we had supposed he had been originally heading.

We soon come to see that his *digressions* are not beside the point. Because he regards all forms of knowledge as part and parcel of the one thing, these digressions usually *are* the point. For instance in *The Principles of Art* he wants to understand what a work of art *is* and what we mean by *artistic expression*. But he also knows that art is part of civilisation, and no full account of civilisation can avoid the subject of politics...or, as it might be, music, literature, dance, architecture, mothers-in-law or armed conflict. Collingwood's sheer profusion can at first be unnerving but, as we persevere in reading him, we feel exhilarated and privileged to be following closely the tracks taken by an almost miraculously agile and fertile mind. Of course, this means that trying to give an outline of Collingwood, or an introduction to his thought, in a single chapter of a book such as this is a virtually impossible task. I think the only way to present him is by copying his method – that is allowing my quotations of him to retain their natural *synoptic* character.

We must start somewhere, and so let us turn to *The Principles of Art.* Collingwood makes an important distinction between what he calls *magic* art and *amusement* art. Magic art is an artwork created for a purpose, as when people we injudiciously describe as *primitive* fashion the image of a bison on the wall of a cave or when they perform a rain dance. Amusement art, when we have too much of it, leads inevitably, says Collingwood to the decline of the civilisation which perpetrates it. That was his conclusion in the paragraph just quoted on Plato and the demise of Greece and Rome.

On the character of magic art, Collingwood goes to great lengths to disprove the notions of such as J.G. Frazer in *The Golden Bough.* Frazer thought that magic art, primitive art, the art of peoples he described as *savages*, was a form of failed science. The savage performed his artistic rain dance, said Frazer, in order to make it rain. Collingwood ridiculed this view:

> "A servant girl in my father's house, when I was a boy, would never light a fire or put on a kettle without saying to it *Burn up fire!* or *Boil up kettle!* Without that ritual, she would not have expected the fire to burn or the kettle to boil. But, simple country lass though she was, and deplorably superstitious, she would have laughed at you had you suggested that the charm would act if the fire was clumsily laid or the kettle unskilfully placed upon it."

He goes on to provide a more convincing analysis of the magic rituals of the *savage:*

"He appears to think that in addition to what we should call *practical* means towards achieving success when hunting or fishing, it is necessary to practise *ritual* means also. He will not hunt or fish or plough without performing ceremonies intended to bring about some indispensable part of the total result. If he ploughs and sows, he has a ploughing and sowing ritual without which he apparently does not think the seed will grow. It is not that he thinks the ritual efficacious by itself: he would never expect to get a crop simply by performing the ritual without the ploughing and sowing at all; nor does he suppose that the ritual will make good any mistakes he makes in the ploughing and sowing."

Those whom we refer to as *primitives* and *savages* were not fools – whatever anthropologists such as Frazer might have thought. Collingwood has a shot at explaining the function of ritual: it is *to encourage one another*, to produce the right spirit in the community; in, for example, a war dance, it would be the attempt (as our ugly contemporary phrase has it) *to psyche themselves up*.

Collingwood was interested in the reason for, as it might be, the decline and fall of Rome, as it were, in itself. But his view of the nature and purpose of historical study always led him to investigate comparisons with our own times. He first understood what it was that precisely befell that ancient civilisation and then he asks whether what he discovers is of application to us today. If the Greco-Roman culture collapsed because it replaced its magic art, its practical, useful ritual, with passive, emotionally barren amusement art, is it possible that the roots of our present discontent bear similarities? Indeed this is what he finds:

"We see the corruption of the poor. Until close on the end of the 19th century, the rustic population of England had an art of its own, rooted in the distant past but still alive with creative vigour: songs and dances, seasonal feasts and dramas and pageantry, all of magical significance and all organically connected with agricultural work. In a single generation this was wiped out of existence by two causes: the Education Act of 1870 which, as imposing on the countrymen an education modelled on the town-dwellers' standards, was one stage in the slow destruction of English rural life by the dominant industrial and commercial class; and secondly the agricultural depression which between 1870 and 1900 wrecked the prosperity of the English agricultural population.

"Then came amusement art. Football – mushroom amusement growth of what had till lately been a ritual practised on feast days in north country towns – came first; then came the cinema and the wireless; and the poor throughout the country went amusement mad. But another event was happening at the same time. Increased production combined with the breakdown of economic organisation led to the appearance of an unemployed class, forced unwillingly into a parasitical condition, deprived of the magical arts in which their grandfathers took their pleasure fifty years ago, left functionless and aimless in the community, living only to accept *panem et circenses*, the dole and the films."

The accuracy of Collingwood's historical diagnosis is revealed in the final catastrophe with which technology has ensured us through the electronic media and the universal corrupt pervasiveness of advertising. We are seeing again what Collingwood described as Rome's *emotional bankruptcy* and its *drones* in our couch-potatoes, binge drinkers and celebrity addicts as they frenetically scramble for *therapy* for their boredom among the ubiquitous, debased (and overwhelmingly pornographic) connections of the internet and the endless puerile jabber over their portable phones; hardly relieved by blasts of rock music on *Radio Four* every time someone finishes speaking, and whenever anyone scores a boundary on the new, debased form of cricket.

What do we learn from the Roman example and its immediate aftermath?

"The vortex revolved, through manifestations now wholly forgotten except by a few curious scholars, until a new consciousness grew up for which practical life was so interesting that organised amusement was no longer needed. The consciousness of the old civilisation, now bifurcated down to its very foundations, fell to pieces before the onslaught of this new unified consciousness, and theatre and amphitheatre were deserted by a world that had become Christian. The Middle Ages had begun and a new magico-religious art was born: this time an art serving those emotions which went to the invigorating and perpetuating of Christian society."

This did not happen overnight. It began with a very small number of people who took themselves apart from the corrupt way of life: they found little communities, some went into the desert and there was the beginning of that great productive revolution which we know as monasticism. There was work and prayer and fellowship. Beside these things, the tawdry satisfactions of bread and circuses could not compete. Gradually, a new civilisation was born: the great cathedrals, plainchant, the European parish system, the revival of agriculture hand in hand with the renewal of learning in the first universities – which, let us remember, were Christian foundations where theology was Queen of the Sciences. The world put away childish things.

What do we learn? Sometimes it seems we have learnt nothing – except our fantastical belief in *progress* even after the experience of the 20th century which produced more deaths in wars than those in all the preceding centuries added together:

"In the latter 19th century, the idea of progress became almost an article of faith. This conception was a piece of sheer metaphysics derived from evolutionary naturalism and foisted upon history by the temper of the age."

Collingwood's ideas about what constitutes historical knowledge and the means by which we set about attaining it were revolutionary: moreover he put his ideas on method to practical use in all his archaeological work and, as we shall see, with brilliant results in his attempt to understand the history of philosophy:

> "The past which an historian studies is not a dead past, but a past which in some sense is still living in the present. All history is the history of thought. You are thinking historically when you say about anything, *I see what the person who made this (wrote this, used this, designed this etc) was thinking.* Until you can say that, you may be trying to think historically but you are not succeeding."

The historian's task is to ask of anything he comes across in the course of his work – a document, an implement, a tool, a weapon of war etc – *What precisely was going on in the mind of the person who wrote, used or fought with this?*

To take a particular example, how can we decide whether Caesar intended merely a punitive raid on Britain or to conquer the country? Collingwood answers:

> "There is, of course, no evidence to speak of except that contained in Caesar's own narrative. There he never says what he meant by his invasions of Britain. It is the fact of his silence which constitutes our chief evidence as to what his intention was. Whatever he meant to bring about, his intention was one which he decided to conceal from his readers. I then compared the strength of his expeditionary force with that of the army sent over by Claudius nearly a century later, and this settled it. Caesar must have intended no mere punitive expedition or demonstration of force, like that of his German expedition of 55BC, but the complete conquest of the country.

This view of mine may be mistaken; but future historians will have to reckon with the question I have raised and either accept my answer or produce a better one.

"People who do not understand historical thinking, but are obsessed by scissors and paste, will say, *It is useless to raise the question, because if your only information comes from Caesar, and Caesar has not told you his plans, you can never know what they were...*

"These are the people who, if they met you one Saturday afternoon with a fishing-rod, creel and camping stool, walking towards the river, would ask, *Going fishing?*

"And I suppose that if they were serving on a jury when someone was tried for attempted murder because he had put arsenic in his wife's tea on Monday and cyanide of potassium in her coffee on Tuesday, and on Wednesday broke her spectacles with a revolver bullet and knocked a piece out of her right ear with another on Thursday, and now pleaded not guilty, they would press for his acquittal because, as he never admitted that he meant to murder her, there could be no evidence that he did mean to."

Collingwood describes beautifully what exactly the historian is doing when he is studying his subject:

"The historian's thought is a perfectly genuine experi-ence, but what he is experiencing is what is going on in his mind now; in so far as he places it, as it were, at arm's length from him in the past, he is misconceiving it; he is arranging in imaginary pigeon-holes of past time what is actually all present and not past at all. And this does not imply that he is making historical mistakes about the past. There *is* no past, except for a person involved in the historical mode of experience; and for him the past is what he carefully and critically thinks it to be. He makes no mistake *qua* historian: the only mistake he makes is the philosophical mistake of arranging in the past what is actually all present experience. The historian is master in his own house; it is a house inhabited by all historians and it consists not of ideas about history but of history itself.

"History today is no longer a scissors and paste affair. Instead of repeating statements accepted on the testimony of authorities, the historian of today makes his own statements on his own authority according to what he finds the evidence in his possession to prove when he analyses it with a certain question in his mind."

I think the most important aspect of Collingwood's entire output is that in which he went on to apply this radical method to the study of philosophy, insisting that metaphysics has always been an historical science: that is to say, the history of philosophy is the history of the absolute presuppositions which have been held in the different historical periods and which change over time.

"Metaphysics has always been an historical science; but metaphysicians have not always been fully aware of the fact."

There is no timeless definition of human nature as Hume and the positivists thought. And the absolute presuppositions of metaphysicians are not timeless truths, as for instance, Kant thought, but presuppositions based on the concurrent understanding of physics. For example, Collingwood demonstrated that Kant's own metaphysics is relevant to a three hundred years period from the time of Newton onwards, but that these presuppositions will not fit with modern physics: for instance, *Every event has a cause* does not apply in the realm of quantum mechanics.

Most of the conceptual confusion which arises in philosophical analysis comes about because philosophers have failed to distinguish between propositions and presuppositions. We do not, as first the Positivists and then the Logical

Positivists vainly believed, come to know that the world of experience is a unity susceptible to scientific investigation simply by *observing* the world: on the contrary, that the world of experience *is* such a unity is an absolute presupposition. As Collingwood says:

> "The priority which presuppositions exercise over propositions is a *logical* priority."

He points out the usually overlooked connection between metaphysics and the health, progress and even the survival of any civilization, and he does this with particular reference to the Greeks:

> "When Aristotle says that God did not create the world, this means that the existence of nature is not a presupposition of natural science but simply an observed fact... When Aristotle described it as a fact discovered by the use of the senses, therefore, he was falling into a metaphysical error. For his own science of nature, no less than any other, the thing was in fact an absolute presupposition. This metaphysical error was corrected by Christianity. Here again it will be seen Aristotle failed in his metaphysical analysis; and his failure was not limited to himself alone; the metaphysical mistake which he made was a commonplace of Greek thought. And since metaphysics is inseparable, as regards success or failure, from ordinary thinking, this breakdown of Greek metaphysics implied a breakdown of Greek science....And because science and civilization, organized thought in its theoretical and practical forms, stand or fall together, the metaphysical error which killed pagan science killed pagan civilization with it."

The doctrine which supplied the metaphysical corrective was the doctrine of the Trinity and its relation to natural science. It is, no less, the doctrine of the Trinity which makes natural science possible. With specific reference to *The Athanasian Creed,* Collingwood says:

"By believing in the Father they meant (always with reference solely to the procedures of natural science) absolutely presupposing that there is a world of nature which is always and indivisibly one world. By believing in the Son they meant always absolutely presupposing that the one natural world is nevertheless a multiplicity of natural realms. By believing in the Holy Ghost they meant absolutely presupposing that the world of nature, throughout its entire fabric, is a world not merely of things but of events or movements.

"These presuppositions *must* be made, they said, by anyone who wished to be saved; saved, that is to say, from the moral and intellectual bankruptcy, the collapse of science and civilization, which was overtaking the pagan world."

Relentlessly, Collingwood exposes the mistake of regarding absolute presuppositions as propositions throughout the history of modern philosophy. In the 19th century this error took the form of Positivism. For example,

"Mill, like a true positivist, did not possess the idea of an absolute presupposition. He thought that what he called the uniformity of nature was an empirical proposition, a generalization about matters of fact."

The Positivists were succeeded in the 20th century by the Logical Positivists who made the same mistake:

"If somebody has mistaken suppositions for propositions, who is it that has made the mistake? I answer, *Mr Ayer*. I do not mean that he initiated the mistake; I have already shown how Mill (and Aristotle) made it before him; I mean only that he has adopted it. The importance of Mr Ayer's work on the subject, again not exclusively his own: (the credit must be shared by a considerable group of so called Logical Positivists) lies in the fact that he has not only made the mistake, he has also refuted it. But he has not abandoned it."

Collingwood then begins a ruthless and brilliant assault on modern Positivism which he exposes as an attack on reason itself:

"The suspicion that resentment, not reason, may afford the true motive of the neo-Positivists' anti-metaphysics is confirmed by the way in which we find them conceiving the relation between metaphysics and natural science. They seem to think of metaphysics as *malicious* towards science (the word is Earl Russell's borrowed from Mr Santayana) and the fear that unless metaphysics is destroyed it will destroy natural science. This implies a complete misreading of the present-day situation...

"The doctrine of the Logical Positivists that metaphysical principles are nonsensical will involve the bankruptcy of all thinking in which any use is made of absolute presuppositions; that is to say, the bankruptcy of all science. Any attack on metaphysics is an attack on the foundations of science."

The error, and perhaps the malice, is all on the side of the Positivists. While denying the meaningfulness of metaphysics, they themselves depended on absolute presuppositions – which is what metaphysics *is*. Their so called Verification Principle – that all meaningful propositions are either analytic (true in virtue of the meanings of the words alone and on pain of contradiction) or empirical (based on observation) – is not itself either analytic or empirical. In other words, the Verification Principle fails its own test. It is in fact the Logical Positivists' absolute presupposition – an example of the very metaphysics they deny.

Collingwood was one of the first to detect the ideological animus in the 1930s Logical Positivists against all traditional values:

"Can it be that we are back once more in the atmosphere of the 18th century, listening to the cry *Ecrasez l'infame*? Is this haste with tumbrel and blade the outcome of a genuine desire to understand metaphysics – an enterprise which to quote Kant – *cannot be indifferent to humanity,* or is the outcome of a desire (not a rare desire, it must be admitted) to belittle what one cannot share and destroy what one cannot understand?

"The notions of the Positivists concerning ethics and theology have nothing to do with what the great moral philosophers and the great theologians have taught under those names. They are simply the foolish ideas many of us invented for ourselves or picked them up from foolish parents or foolish nurses when we were small children. Many of us again look back on our childhood with bitter humiliation and resentment; in these cases, if our child-hood has been passed in what is called a virtuous and reli-gious home, the resentment attaches itself to what we (perhaps wrongly) believe to have been taught there, and *Ecrasez l'infame* becomes a motive for rejecting in later life with contumely, and with argument, if we are trained to argue, the traces of that real or supposed teaching still discernible in ourselves."

Collingwood saw more clearly than any of his time the acute danger to our society and civilization posed by the delib-erate misunderstanding of metaphysics and its relation to scientific thought:

"The danger to science from anti-metaphysics is more serious now than it has ever been before."

And yet, seventy years after his great *Essay on Metaphysics* most people think, if they think about these things at all, that the positivistic outlook stands for clarity of thought, while metaphysics is just a byword for superstition. The antidote to this most dangerous misconception is to read Collingwood:

160

"To say that metaphysics deals with God, freedom and immortality is to invite the ridicule of everyone who prides himself on being what William James called *tough-minded* or in the slang of today, *hard-boiled*. It suggests to people of this kind that metaphysics is a game in which senile sentimentalists play at taking seriously the old wives' tales they heard when they were children. But I have shown that, interpreted historically, the proposition, *God exists* takes its place not among old wives' tales but among the absolute presuppositions of science and civilization. Similar interpretations could be given, granted adequate historical equipment, for the beliefs in human freedom and human immortality; which, thus metaphysically expounded, are by no means the mere wish-fulfillment fantasies for which they are too often taken."

He concludes with a warning – the same warning given by T.E. Hulme when he spoke of the greatest danger to a people as *being themselves penetrated by the ideas and notions of their most bitter enemies.* To give a tragic example from the present day in this country, we might reflect on the abject degree to which the Church of England has imbibed the rampant secularism of the last forty years. As Collingwood concludes,

"Civilisations sometimes perish because they are forcibly broken up by the armed attack of enemies without or revolutionaries within; but never from this cause alone. Such attacks never succeed unless the thing that is attacked is weakened by doubt as to whether the end which it sets before itself, the form of life which it tries to realize, is worth achieving. On the other hand, this doubt is quite capable of destroying a civilization without any help whatever. If the people who share a civilization are no longer on the whole convinced that the form of life which it tries to realize is worth realizing, nothing can save it."

The task of reconstruction is as necessary as it is daunting:

"The gravity of the peril lies especially in the fact that so few recognize any peril to exist. When Rome was in danger, it was the cackling of the sacred geese that saved the Capitol. I am only a professorial goose, consecrated with a cap and gown and fed at a college table; but cackling is my job, and cackle I will."

Collingwood was an inspirational teacher with the ability to illuminate any topic to which he applied his mind and to dispel mistaken and foolish conceptions wherever they arose. Let us take, for instance, the case of the Greek gods. Modern types look back on the classical era and find in the Greeks a bewildering naivety: how could such an intelligent people come to believe that the gods were actual representations abiding on Mount Olympus from where, from time to time, they descended to interfere in the destinies of men? Collingwood explains that the Greeks did not in fact hold this belief at all:

"Their habit of representing their gods in vividly realised human form was not a piece of theology, it was a piece of poetry. When they described or portrayed Aphrodite, for example, they did not think they were describing or portraying a non-natural woman who, by the exercise of something like will, but a superhuman will, brought about the various events which together make up her realm, namely the events connected with sexual reproduction. They did not think they were portraying a person who controlled or produced these events; they thought they were portraying these events themselves."

Collingwood illuminates this point brilliantly with a particular example:

"In the *Hippolytus* of Euripides, a young man is cruelly done to death because he refuses to gratify the incestuous passion of his stepmother. In terms of poetry, his destruction is compassed by a quasi-human person called Aphrodite in the execution of her vengeance upon him for refusing, not then only but always, in sexual intercourse; a refusal which she regards as insulting to herself as the patron of sex. In order to achieve her vengeance, this goddess deprives his stepmother first of her happiness and self-respect and then of her life, and robs his father both of wife and of son, making him his son's murderer." What are we to make of all this? Collingwood says.

"Simple-minded modern readers can hardly restrain their indignation; allow themselves strong language about the low morality of Greek religious ideas. But they are deceived. The story of the *Hippolytus* would be exactly the same if you left the goddess out. Here it is:

"Once upon a time, there was a young man who had a horror of women. To persuade himself that these was nothing wrong with him, he devoted himself to blood sports. His mother was dead, and his father married again, a nice young woman, good looking and of good family, though there were odd stories about them... Well, as luck would have it, or perhaps it was that queer streak in her family, she fell violently in love with her stepson. She was almost dying of love when her old nurse found out about it and persuaded her to speak to the young man. He refused her with such disgust that she didn't know what to do. So she committed suicide, leaving a letter for her husband saying that it was because her stepson had made love to her. The old man believed it; so he had him murdered. The moral is that sex is a thing about which you cannot afford to make mistakes."

Because our simple-minded modern person fails in his imagination to recognise that the Greeks' practice of personifying their gods is poetry, he thereby fails to understand that the story is about sexual morality and sexual psychology.

Collingwood was voluminous. It might be said of him what Mahler said of the symphony – that it *contains worlds.* He possessed one of the finest minds of the 20th century. L.O. Mink aptly described him as, *the best known neglected thinker of our time.* And he is so penetrating, so illuminating: his arguments affect us with the reassuring certainty of bolts being firmly slammed home. I should like to end with something Collingwood said about one of T.S. Eliot's short poems, first because Eliot also features prominently in this book but, more importantly, because this is the most focussed attention on a piece of literature one could hope to find. It is simply the model of what all good criticism should be:

"I do not know how many readers of Mr Eliot's poem *Sweeney among the Nightingales* have the least idea of what precisely the situation is which the poet is depicting. I have never heard or read any expression of such an idea. Sweeney has dropped asleep in a restaurant, vaguely puzzled by the fact that the Convent of the Sacred Heart next door has reminded him of something, he cannot tell what. A wounded Heart, and waiting, husbandless, women. As he snores all through the second verse, a prostitute in a long cloak comes and sits on his knees, and at that moment, he dreams the answer.

"It is Agamemnon's cry – *O I am wounded mortally to the heart* – wounded to death at his homecoming by the false wife he had left behind. He wakes, stretching and laughing (tilting the girl off his knee) as he realises that in the queer working of his mind, the hooded, husbandless nuns and the cloaked, husbandless girl, waiting there like a spider for her prey, are both Klytaemnestra, the faithless wife who threw her cloak (the net of death) round her lord and stabbed him.

"I quote this case because I had known and enjoyed the poem for years before I saw that this was what it was all about; and nevertheless I understood enough to value it highly. And it was not until a few days later, after I had written these words, that I recognised the poem's phrase *gloomy Orion* as a borrowing from Marlowe's *Dido* – another tragedy about a husbandless woman."

Chapter Eight

C.H. Sisson (1914–2003)

Charles Hubert Sisson was born in Bristol in 1914 and died in Langport, Somerset in 2003. He attended only the state elementary school and then went on to Bristol University to read English and Philosophy. He gained a small travelling studentship which enabled him to spend a year in France and Germany in the 1930s – and he saw something of the rise of Hitler. He joined the Civil Service and rose to the rank of Permanent Undersecretary in the Ministry of Labour.

Sisson was a classicist and a linguist fluent in the European languages, so typically the army sent him off to spend the war in India. Upon his return and for the rest of his life he combined his work in the Ministry with the vocation of a man of letters: poet, critic, novelist, philosopher and translator – particularly of Horace and Heine and also of what many regard as the best modern version of Dante's *Divine Comedy*. He wrote a profound novel *Christopher Homm* which originated a literary device – telling the story backwards – and which has been much copied.

First of all he was a perceptive critic, writing for small magazines and subsequently having his criticism collected and published by *Carcanet Press*. It should be said right away that he did not work as a critic because he liked carping or pulling people down; but because he was passionately and humanely concerned for the advancement of the best. Like Eliot, his motive was always *to purify the dialect of the tribe.* He quickly established a reputation for exposing humbug – even when the humbug was being spouted by a national treasure or someone who would now disgustingly be regarded as a *cultural icon*. For example, Walter Bagehot is regarded very widely as the expert on the monarchy and the constitution. Sisson begins by showing him for the shallow snob he was. Bagehot wrote:

> "Let an accomplished man try what seems to him most obvious, most certain, most palpable in intellectual matters upon the housemaid and the footman, and he will find that what he says seems so unintelligible, confused and erroneous – that his audience think him mad and wild."

Sisson comments:

> "One can imagine the servants at Bagehot's Herd's Hill: *Mr Walter do say some things!*"

He gives us Bagehot's actual opinions about the monarchy:

> "Walter Bagehot attributed importance to the monarchy but it was an importance of an inferior kind. The Queen was *dignified* in his phraseology: that meant she was not much good. She was for fools to goggle at. So Trooping the Colour must be regarded as a leg-show of guardsmen, the Crown as a bauble and the Coronation itself as something for the illustrated papers."

Sisson goes on to develop his criticism of Bagehot and to inform us about the true function of the Queen: she is no mere ornament, no vacuous *dignity*, she does rule over us.

> "The Queen rules through her ministers and she does not rule any the less for that. The minister does not attend to the details of his department's administration. The minister has one inalienable function which is to secure the coherence of his department. The Queen has one inalienable function which is to secure the coherence of her country."

And he concludes by explaining why the monarchy is vital for the health of the nation:

"The final safeguard of our unity is a single Person present on the throne by hereditary right and form of law. If we depart from that, we admit the legitimacy of faction. No doubt it is only in the most desperate troubles, such as we pray we shall be preserved from, that that Person would present herself to us so directly. But it is well that we should not allow sloppy ideas to obscure what would be our duty in such an emergency."

That the monarchy is not really important is the underlying assumption of all our politicians. So they follow Bagehot and Sisson's criticism applies to them too:

"Bagehot's view was that the paraphernalia of the constitution of Church and Crown and Parliament did not matter so long as the business of the day was done. It is a point of view so familiar to us that it is accepted by most people without a thought. The unimportance of everything except the promotion of manufacture and the circulation of money now seems to be as unquestionable a truth as ever our former constitutional principles were. Indeed it has replaced those constitutional principles."

Sisson did not much care for airy talk about the writer's *style,* but if there is a word for his own method, it is ironic. His collected literary essays are titled *The Avoidance of Literature.* Here are a few examples of the sort of literature he sought to avoid:

"E.M. Forster's credo is an amused disowning of everything that is not himself, who sees himself as one of *the sensitive, the considerate and the plucky.* Readers of his novels will know who is meant – the cosy snobs of *Howard's End* and the picnickers in *A Passage to India.*"

Forster, says Sisson, approves of those who

"...produce literature and art, or they do disinterested scientific research, are creative in their private lives and even found religions – which you might have thought, on Forster's principles, was not a very good thing to do. It is important for him that all culture is seen to belong to the gang and his aberration extends to claiming Dante as belonging to his set on the grounds that he placed Brutus and Cassius in the lowest circle of hell *because they had chosen to betray their friend Julius Caesar rather than their country, Rome* – though in fact they were put there because they had betrayed their Master – the type in that circle being Judas Iscariot."

Forster wrote, *All the great creative actions, all the decent human relations, occur during the intervals when force has not managed to come to the front.*
Sisson comments:

"The Crucifixion, for example?"

He has only contempt for the Bloomsbury group:

"A gang of pacifist aesthetes taking their pleasures seriously behind the high walls of Garsington while rough hewn men were fighting and dying on the Western Front."

Dominant among the poets when Sisson was a young man was W.H. Auden. Sisson writes about him and his friends in his book *English Poetry 1900–1950* and says:

"It was the day of Auden, Spender and of Day-Lewis who had not yet become a professor. It seemed that to be a poet you had to feel the woes of the working classes more than anyone else's. These classes had woes, for it was a time of great unemployment and poverty. But I could not help noticing that it was not from a world I inhabited – which actually contained working people – that these St Georges came riding to the relief of the poor. They came, it seemed, from what they represented as the closed middle class of *majors, vicars, lawyers, doctors, advertisers and maiden aunts.* (Their maiden aunts, not mine) whom they made a special point of denouncing.

"It was perhaps unfortunate therefore that, on leaving Oxford, Auden went, after a year in Germany, to teach in such an establishment as The Downs School, near Malvern. The protective covering must have been pretty thick there. It is not very brave to shout *Boo!* to your maiden aunt from such a hideout, and to associate yourself vaguely with the threats of death and revolution, and of the irruption of a rough proletariat turning nasty on the dole. The old combination of revolution and privileged self-interest – the old Whig formula – was the whole tone of that Oxford Communism of the 1930s. The imaginative ambition of Auden and his friends was, as Auden himself said, *to hunger, work illegally and be anonymous* – but in real life none of these things was much in their line."

These 1930s Left wing poets were the natural successors to Forster and the rest of the effete crowd at Garsington:

"They taught that one should be ashamed of being well-off and I felt that I was being called to be ashamed too because, though I was not well-off, I had to admit I was not a proletarian. About the same time I began to meet people who belonged to the social world of these three poets and who like them were beginning to drip the tears of socialism. When they spoke of the workers, it was as if they were speaking of people in some far off fairyland or alternatively of a remote race of South Sea Islanders or of a favourite breed of beetle. Nonetheless, they had it seemed the only language in which one could speak with indignation of the lot of the unemployed. Moreover, it was taken as of course that they alone had those treasures of intellect which, rightly spread around, were bound to result in a cure of every economic and social evil."

We know that Auden escaped actual tribulations by leaving the country and contrived to spend the Second World War in New York from where he denounced his former countrymen for their having lived through *a low, dishonest decade.* The litterateurs' humbug continued even after the war had started. Sisson says:

> "There is a good deal of comedy about Cyril Connolly's moralisings. The war, he says*, was being fought for culture.* That would explain the attitude of the grateful fighter pilots."

Sisson preferred Eliot, Hulme, Wyndham Lewis and Ezra Pound for what he saw as their realistic attitude towards the world crisis:

> "What Pound exposed in *The Cantos* is the monstrous aberration of a world in which reality is distorted, down to a detail never so comprehensively indicated before, by the pull of a fictitious money. It is a noble subject and may well be the only possible one for a long poem in our age."

Pound was famous for his ability to spot what Sisson called *sham antique* and Eliot described as the decadent activity *to summon the spectre of a rose or follow an antique drum.* And he quotes with glee Pound's parody of Housman's characteristic lugubriousness and his mechanical rhythm:

> Come tumtum Greek Ulysses, come
> Caress these shores with me
> The windblown seas have wet my bum
> *And here the beer is free.*

There was something not quite incarnated about the *The Shropshire Lad.* As Sisson says:

> "Housman himself was urban, precise and better-suited to his final destiny of drinking port at High Table than to

rollicking with the lads at Ludlow Fair."

The trick of passing off titillation as high art is not original to our own times. Sisson commented more than half a century ago:

"The fuss about Beardsley's drawings was of a low origin, and we are not yet at the end of the period when money is to be made out of giving prominence to just a little more obscenity than people in general are accustomed to. It matters little that the moral indignation is now always on the side of the Wilde's or the Beardsley's, or rather of those who, however devoid of wit as of draughtsmanship, are their sociological successors."

He refers to:

"...what is called the intellectual atmosphere, meaning that which prevails in the tracts between literature and fornication."

One of the few poets even to get so much as a mention in state schools today is Wilfred Owen, and this of course is because he is used as a weapon in the antiwar industry, the *Blackadder* country of lions led by donkeys. Sisson asks us to recall Owen's saying:

The poetry is in the pity.

And he comments:

"The sentence about English poetry not yet being fit to speak of heroes connotes an ill-placed progressivism. Were there any grounds for thinking that the language of Chaucer and Shakespeare was taking a turn for the better, so that one day, if it continued to get good reports, it would be able to speak of matters which were above the heads of those beginners? *Might, majesty, dominion and power* and other Prayer Book trash: none of these things is serious compared with what Wilfred is going to say. Anyway, what right has a poet to say that he is not concerned with poetry?"

So where was the authentic poetic note being sounded in the early part of the last century? In answering this question Sisson repudiates the usual suggestion that original work in poetry is the special contribution of political radicals:

"It is an odd fact that, in a century in which it has, on the whole, paid writers to trade under a left-wing label, so few of the major figures have done so. For some of the most eminent figures – one need go no further than Eliot, Yeats, Pound, Lawrence, Hulme and Wyndham Lewis – it has been necessary to enter special apologies to explain how people so recalcitrant to the main stream of intellectual prejudice can be accepted as intellectually respectable in spite of it all."

In fact literature is a rare commodity and people do not readily look for it:

"Those who consider that the day's newspaper or the winner of the latest poetry prize is more to be considered than the master texts should reflect soberly on Dante's submission to Virgil. So should those who think that the most exalted matter can be dressed up in the language of journalism and of the contemporary poetry trade. If Dante and Catullus, Horace or Raleigh or some equivalent figures are not of actual importance to you in terms of pleasure and enlightenment, then literature – the designation of the permanent element in man – is not what you are interested in as you turn to the weeklies and the Sunday supplements. It is thought proper that the poet should be put to work in a culture factory – say the English department of a university – or at promoting the legitimate diversions of highbrows through The Arts

Council. All this is due to a theory of work, not to a theory of art."

The work of the poet is not so much romantic effusiveness as a craft which has to be learnt and practised:

"The Romantic is, so to speak, a holidaymaker with vague thoughts of luxurious beauty. The Classic is a man no less serious than the fisherman mending his nets. His preoccupations do not leave him. He does not turn aside for beauty. No good writer does. The distinction between *Classic* and *Romantic* is merely the distinction between good writing and bad."

And this craft is:

"An absolute ruthlessness in taking what seems good and rejecting what seems bad is required in writing as in reading."

On his way home from his office in St James, Sisson would call into churches. He records:

"You might as well know that one Sunday afternoon when I was thirty-nine I was baptised in a small brick church. The approach to these mysteries was something like giving oneself up to the police. I had committed the crime – if it is one – of yielding to the persuasions of the Creed... There is a modern mind which finds it impossible to justify joining the Church. What makes St Augustine so attractive is that he was acquainted with something very much like the modern mind, and turned his back on it."

Sisson was a serious Christian. I will quote a few paragraphs from his autobiography *On The Lookout* which say, better than I can, what being a Christian and an Anglican meant to him:

"The most sickening form of defence used by the apologists for the church's decay is to suggest that the general dissolution is merely evidence of freedom of conscience, or even of unworldliness. But Laud mounting the scaffold or Cranmer going out to be burned were no more worldly than the bishops who consume long hours on indifferent committees or at ladies' coffee mornings. They were merely much more deeply implicated in the society of their times so that they could not choose but to take decisions which led them into trouble and locked them in unending struggle with the most brilliant and powerful men of their time. A coffee morning is not, of its nature, a more spiritual thing than a council of state.

"There is no meaning except in terms of a time and a place. If one could understand, it would be at one altar in a stone building, in such a place, at perhaps eight o'clock on a Sunday morning. If there were no Sacraments, there would be nothing. If there were not England, there would be no church for me who happen to have been born here. I am an Anglican.

"It is the Sacraments which tie one to the world; without them one would wander unassured in a sort of limbo which is no doubt the impersonal world of the mechanism with no subjective part. This may be hell. It is what the religionists of the technological world are trying to imitate, as artists were once thought to imitate the creation of God. The Sacramental life is the alternative. In practice this means joining people not of your choosing, but who in some sort have chosen what you have chosen, and turning up at inconvenient times to perform a corporate act with them. The theology of it is that you have not chosen at all, but been chosen, so it is none of your business whether the silly sheep who are with you have caught sight of the Shepherd. Have you caught sight of him yourself? My woolly head is buried in the sides of the other sheep.

"At any rate when I joined the church it was because it seemed to me that the world was as the Creed said it was. Nothing was excluded; one was merely removing a prejudice which concealed the miraculous nature of the creation. People talk about the Christian doctrine of marriage as if it were a moral rule invented to crush tender feelings and healthy appetites. Actually it is a fact about the nature of man and woman. You can do something different; all but saints in some sort do. The fact will remain, all you can do is deflect your mind from it, and our wobbly minds find it pleasant to be deflected. It is so with the Creed. It says what it is; it does not say anything else. No one can surprise you with a fact that is inconsistent with it, because there are no such facts. The ordinary modern objections to the church are simply irrelevant.

"I feel none of the difficulties some eminent churchmen appear to find about accepting those articles of the Creed which appear to conflict with the latest news from the laboratories. I see nothing to tempt me in the half-way houses which are now so popular both in the church and outside, where people who find the Creed insufferable have no difficulty in believing in various panaceas for misplaced hopes."

He criticises both those who disparage Christianity out of mere ignorance and the ignorant clergy who would lead them:

"People think that there is something sacred about an individual opinion, however ill-informed."

Individual opinion has become a secular dogma and *Everyone has a right to their* (sic) *own opinion* has come to mean that every opinion is as good as any other. Absolute relativism rules OK?

"The fashion is for clerics who would teach before they have learned and who excuse themselves by pretending that they need no more than the media-soaked language of their more ignorant parishioners."

Sisson contrasts the way Christianity was understood and what it counted for in the 16th century with the soppy plea for excuses into which it has now declined:

"It was not very nice that people should burn one another for their faith, or that archbishops should be executed for their political devotion to their Sovereign, but these things were done because, at the time when they were done, there was not the present facility in extracting from theological conceptions all trace of practical meaning."

The Creed informs us that it is God who is at the centre of all things, including the centre and origin of all meaning. Thought must begin with this understanding and not with speculative epistemology which starts with the word *I*. So Sisson exposed the philosophical nonsense that results when we start our philosophising where Descartes and the modern age starts it – with itself, with myself:

"There is of course a sense in which *I* is self-evident. But it is a pretty silly sense, a sort of tautology. *I* is merely the fact of the assertion being made. It does not get one out of the prison of solipsism. But when we say *I exist,* what we are really hoping is that there are other *I's.* If we do not mean that, we do not mean anything. Indeed there could hardly be such a thing as meaning."

This is essentially Wittgenstein's private language refutation of Cartesian Dualism in *Philosophical Investigations* – but Sisson said it first.

He wrote poetry for most of his life and published seven collections, the last of these poems composed when he was in his eighties. One might quote any one from hundreds:

Easter

One good crucifixion and he rose from the dead
He knew better than to wait for age
To nibble his intellect
And depress his love

Out in the desert the sun beats and the cactus
Prickles more fiercely than any in his wilderness
And his forty days
Were merely monastic.

What he did on the cross was not more
Than others have done for less reason
And the resurrection you could take for granted.
What is astonishing is that he came here at all
Where no one ever came voluntarily before.

The language is so lean and spare. Following his own strictures, there is no *turning aside for beauty*. In fact, not turning aside for beauty is the only way to attain to beauty: not romantic but classic.

The Evidence

If you had hopes once they have turned to reason
If you had reason it has turned to evidence:
The evidence is against you.

Divine Poems

Work without hope is the best recipe
For a harmless life, if any life can be harmless
That is born of woman and goes back into the slot.
There was one, harmless, who came that way

A broken spirit, a contrite heart
Are acceptable, taken together

But the native spirit that I have broken
Does not go with contrition.

I can no more be contrite, God
Than I can understand your magnificence
A creeper here, a boaster there
My conscience is under the tarmac.

Abjection is also a vice
For there is nothing which could be abject
In nothing, which is what I am
Stamped with the maker's image.

Sisson lived for a time in Sevenoaks and was churchwarden at St Nicholas' where John Donne had been Vicar. This traditional Anglican church was taken over by a happy-clappy parson who achieved an injunction on the following poem with the result that Sisson could not publish it until the parson had died – the happy clappy-clapped out at last:

A Letter to John Donne

I understand you well enough, John Donne
First, that you were a man of ability
Eaten by lust and by the love of God
Then, that you crossed the Sevenoaks High Street
As Rector of St Nicholas:
I am of that parish
To be a man of ability is not much
You may see them on the Sevenoaks platform any day
Eager men with despatch cases
Whom ambition drives as they drive the machine
Whom the certainty of meticulous operation
Pleasures as a morbid sex a heart of stone.
That you should have spent your time in the corruption of courts
As these in that of cities, gives you no place among us:
Ability is not even the game of a fool

But the click of a computer operating in a waste
Your cleverness is dismissed from the suit
Bring out your genitals and your theology.
What makes you familiar is this dual obsession;
Lust is not what the rutting stag knows
It is to take Eve's apple and to lose
The stag's paradisal look:
The love of God comes readily
To those who have most need.
You brought body and soul into this church
Walking there through the park alive with deer
But now what animal has climbed into your pulpit?
One whose pretension is that the fear
Of God has heated him into a spirit
An evaporated man no physical ill can hurt.
Well might you hesitate at the Latin gate
Seeing such apes denying the church of God:
I am grateful particularly that you were not a saint
But extravagant in bed or in your shroud.
You would understand that in the presence of folly
I am not sanctified but angry.
Come down and speak to the men of ability
On the Sevenoaks platform and tell them
That at your St Nicholas the faith
Is not exclusive in the fools it chooses
That the vain, the ambitious and the highly sexed
Are the natural prey of the incarnate Christ.

The Trade

The language fades. The noise is more
Than ever it has been before,
But all the words grow pale and thin
For lack of sense has done them in.

What wonder, when it is for pay
Millions are spoken every day?
It is the number not the sense

That brings the speakers pounds and pence.

The words are stretched across the air
Vast distances from here to there,
Or there to here, it does not matter
So long as there is media chatter.

Turn up the sound and let there be
No talking between you and me:
What passes now for human speech
Must come from somewhere out of reach.

To His Grace the Archbishop of York with recollections of his contribution to the BBC "Sunday" programme 30th December 1984

A shepherd in a northern town
Saw angels just above his head:
"They look like geese to me!" he said
And took his bow and shot one down
"That will do, as I am a sinner
For Mrs Joseph's Christmas dinner!"

He seized the bird and dragged it round
To where the happy couple slept:
"My dears, take this" And as he stepped
Inside the stable, there he found
A baby with a brilliant future.
"It shows," he said "in every feature.

"Why bless my soul," he added laughing,
"Mary, they said you were a virgin!
The truth I said is just emerging
By God, and here it is! A passing
Joke but I mean to keep it up
When I am made an archbishop!

"By mirrors and prevarication

I will proceed, they will like that;
The Creed is rather awkward but
It works, in the imagination.
Nonetheless I put more reliance
On stinks and elementary science.

"God I am sure won't touch my Minster;
He only works in images,
They're harmless, aren't they? What a wheeze!
As soon suppose he'd make a spinster
Into a mum, as that he'd trade
In medals for the Fire Brigade.

"Pull up the ladder, Jack, the rungs
Are words I used in my ascent.
The Word is nothing different
And earlier ages got it wrong.
After all, Athanasius
Can hardly count as one of us!"

Vigil and Ode for St George's Day

Yet may time's treasure still remain
Until it quietly ebbs away
Beyond our knowledge, England's day
I cannot help it for the pain

Of her demise is more than all
The mind can suffer for the death
Of any creature that draws breath,
And should her time come round again

Our dust will stir, not to a drum
Or any folly men devise
But to the peace which once our eyes
Met in her fields, or else in some

Of her best children, from the first.

All this is folly too and yet
Rather than any should forget
Let this sad island be immersed

In raging storm and boiling seas.
Let no man speak for her unless
He speaks too for her gentleness
And it is her he seeks to please.

Sisson was no ivory tower scholar. No poetic recluse. He did not much go in for talking about himself, but perhaps it might be informative to end with a few of his remarks on contemporary society and finally with his typically ironic reflection on his own life. He says:

"Does it matter that we now live in a state in which it is important that Sikhs should publicly exercise their customs but it is thought wrong that a child should be taught the Creed or the Catechism at the public expense?"

He retired early from his position in The Ministry of Labour after publishing three articles in *The Spectator* which were highly critical of the Head of the Civil Service. As long ago as the 1970s, he highlighted what he saw as an enervating feature with which more recently we have become exceptionally familiar:

"The characteristic of the last few years is a growth of the mythology of management. There has been a deliberate and persistent propagation of the idea that management is a new conception of the civil service and an attempt to persuade people that analytical procedures of a kind which have always held an important place at middle executive levels have now been introduced as a startling novelty from the top, and that this is about to produce a new golden age of efficiency."

And he added ruefully:

"It is possible to occupy a top position in a major department in Whitehall without having the capacity to run a tobacco shop."

He never had illusions about Whitehall:

"When I became a civil servant I was put in a room with a man of experience who was doing things about unemployment insurance. I had read Kafka, so I understood all this perfectly."

Collingwood detected an obsession with *progress* developing out of 19th century evolutionary science. Sisson went further:

"The mythology of progress which dominated the 19th century has given way to another which, being still in fashion, is of course not regarded as a mythology at all. The current doctrine recommends change as being a good thing. One of the most alarming prospects of the technological world is the achievement of a society in which change is simultaneous and worldwide, so that the lessons of earlier epochs are expunged before they are understood."

Technological changes affect more than the apparatus of health care:

"In a technocratic world the devices for treating people as things are subtle and far-reaching. The very kindnesses of the great organisation are done without any conversation between consciousnesses. The sick man is taken into hospital and modified as one might modify an engine. The somewhat unfashionable idea that a plague is a visitation of God's wrath respects the being of the sick man in a way which the successive transformations of William Smith into William Smith Mark II and Mark III, does not. The ease of technology will in the end produce a race of diminishing consciousness for whom the only persuasion is by force. The triumph of technology would be to leave people with so little consciousness that they did not notice the change."

And he gave early warning of the cult of the *media personality* and the *celebrity*:

"The method of creating bogus personalities which has become one of the diseases of the age, with every scruffy talker seeking to pass himself off as a fascinating personality."

Long before the coining of the phrase *neo-con* and the excited urge on the parts of western nations to try to create democracies out of ancient tyrannies, as in Afghanistan or comparatively new ones such as Saddam's Iraq, Sisson wrote:

"The word democracy is now so full of air that it is about to burst. Its bursting will not be the end of everything but the recognition in passing of a truth. The religion of democracy is the religion most of them now favour – I mean that sentimentality about vulgar opinion which has come to be regarded as a sacred principle. The only state religion is democracy which is not an actual system of government, such as we all may defend provisionally as the lesser of evils, but an extraordinary heap of superstitions which have taken on all the sacredness of the truth."

And he saw the contradictions involved in social engineering, whether at home or abroad:

"If those who talk most of changing society also talk most of individual liberty, it is merely that they are confused. To make a change is to make other people bend."

So much of the agitated, high-minded talk about *rights* is only hot air:

> "Any reform would have to start by washing away all that rubbish of imaginary rights which are conceived as a sort of metaphysical property of each individual, as if there could be a right which did not impose a duty on some-body else."

The following words were written in 1969 when the burgeoning television talk shows were almost genteel compared with their coarser successors today:

> "Mankind will at last be let down to a level appropriate to their mass imbecility. And no one can say that, with tele-vision, this work is not going forward at commendable speed, so that the families of professional men, where the ordinary wits of a society ought predominantly to be found, think it natural to bring up their families in a welter of sensation to which appropriately enough Freud and Proust form part of the intellectual background; while they themselves suffer instruction in the affairs of the world at the hands of David Frost."

I was privileged to get to know Charles Sisson in 1979 when I was preparing a book of essays for *Blackwells* in defence of *The Book of Common Prayer* and criticising its soon to be published replacement *The Alternative Service Book.* My wife and I used to go to see him in Langport where he lived next to the parish church on top of the only hill for miles. He had a huge window through which your eyes were drawn below to the river winding away to the horizon like the happy ending of an old film.

We might drive out for a pub lunch and pass the churches which he used to visit clandestinely, remove the modern prayer books and hide them and, if he could find copies, replace them in the pews and on the lectern with *The King James Bible* and the real Prayer Book.

This is how he ends the book he titles *On The Lookout: A Partial Autobiography:*

"An old man may be allowed regrets, but they are no more to the point than the hopes of earlier years. One can hardly do better than turn to the visible world, and there I am fortunate. Before my window the fields stretch away to the Dorset hills; the willows, no longer pollarded, have not all been removed. The river flows or overflows among them, according to the season. What it all means, God knows."

Further Reading

Chapter 1

Yale Edition of the Works of Samuel Johnson (Newhaven 1958)

Lives of the English Poets – Samuel Johnson (G.B. Hill edition Oxford 1905)

The Life of Samuel Johnson – James Boswell (Wordsworth Editions 1999)

Samuel Johnson – Walter Jackson Bate (Chatto & Windus 1978)

Samuel Johnson in Grub Street – Edward A. Bloom (Providence R.I. 1957)

Dr Johnson's Dictionary – James H. Sled and Gwin J. Kolb (Chicago 1955)

Chapter 2

Biographia Literaria – S.T. Coleridge (J.M. Dent 1906)

On the Constitution of the Church and State – S.T. Coleridge (J.M. Dent 1972)

Aids to Reflection – S.T. Coleridge (G. Bell & Sons Ltd 1913)

Lay Sermons – S.T. Coleridge (ed R.J. White Princeton and Routledge 1972)

The Table Talk of S.T. Coleridge (ed Carl R. Woodring Princeton and Routledge 1990)

Coleridge's Notebooks, a Selection (ed Seamus Perry OUP 2002)

Coleridge: Early Visions – Richard Holmes (Hodder & Stoughton 1989)

Coleridge: Darker Reflections 1804–1834 – Richard Holmes (Harper Collins 1998)

The Life of Samuel Taylor Coleridge – Rosemary Ashton (Blackwell 1996)

Samuel Taylor Coleridge: A Biographical Study – E.K. Chambers (Oxford 1938)

The Life of Samuel Taylor Coleridge – James Gillman MD (Oxford 1838)

Chapter 3

Apologia Pro Vita Sua – J.H. Newman (Fontana edition 1959)

On the Scope and Nature of University Education – J.H. Newman (J.M. Dent 1915)

The Idea of a University – J.H. Newman (ed I.T. Ker (Oxford 1976)

An Essay in Aid of a Grammar of Assent – J.H. Newman (Oxford 1985)

An Essay on the Development of Christian Doctrine – J.H. Newman (Longmans, Green & Co 1881)

Fifteen Sermons Preached before the University of Oxford – J.H. Newman (Longmans, Green & Co 1881)

John Henry Newman: A Biography – I.T. Ker (Clarendon Press 1988)

The Life of John Henry Newman – W.G. Ward

Chapter 4

The Collected Works of G.K. Chesterton – (Ignatius Press 1987)

St Thomas Aquinas: the Dumb Ox – G.K. Chesterton (Sheed & Ward 1933)

Collected Poems – G.K. Chesterton (Methuen 1927)

The Victorian Age in Literature – G.K. Chesterton (Edgeways Books 2001)

Orthodoxy – G.K. Chesterton (Fontana 1962 edition)

The Everlasting Man – G.K. Chesterton (Ignatius Press 1991 edition)

Eugenics and Other Evils – G.K. Chesterton (Inkling Books 2000)

St Francis of Assisi – G.K. Chesterton (Continuum 2001)

Gilbert Keith Chesterton – Maisie Ward (Sheed & Ward 1944)

Wisdom and innocence: A Life of GKC – Joseph Pearce (Hodder & Stoughton 1996)

Chapter 5

Selected Writings – T.E. Hulme Ed Patrick McGuinness (Carcanet Press 1998)

T.E. Hulme – Michael Roberts (Faber & Faber 1938; Carcanet Press 1982 ed with an introduction by Anthony Quinton)

The Life & Opinions of T.E.Hulme – Alun R. Jones (Gollancz 1960)

The Importance of T.E. Hulme in *Experiments Against Reality p.45-p60* – Roger Kimball (I. R. Dee 2000)

English Poetry 1900–1950: An Assessment p64-p68 – C.H. Sisson (Carcanet Press 1981)

Chapter 6

The Complete Poems and Plays of T.S.Eliot – (Faber & Faber 1969)

Christianity and Culture (comprising *The Idea of a Christian Society (1939)* and *Notes Towards the Definition of Culture (1948)* – T.S. Eliot (Harcourt Brace & Co 1976)

The Sacred Wood – T.S. Eliot (Methuen 1920)

The Use of Poetry and the Use of Criticism – T.S. Eliot (Faber & Faber 1933)

Selected Prose – T.S. Eliot (ed Frank Kermode (Faber and Faber 1975)

Four Quartets: A Selection of Critical Essays ed Bernard Bergonzi (Macmillan 1969)

T.S. Eliot: The Invisible Poet – Hugh Kenner Methuen 1959)

The Achievement of T.S. Eliot – F. O. Mathiessen (OUP 1947)

Words Alone: The Poet T.S. Eliot – Denis Donoghue (Yale 2000)

Chapter 7

An Essay on Philosophical Method – R.G. Collingwood (OUP 1933)

An Essay on Metaphysics – R.G. Collingwood (OUP 1940)

The Idea of History – R.G. Collingwood (ed Jan van der Dussen OUP 2005)

An Autobiography – R.G. Collingwood (OUP 1938)

The Philosophy of Enchantment – R.G. Collingwood (ed David Boucher, Wendy James and Philip Smallwood (Clarendon Press 2005)

The Principles of Art – R.G. Collingwood (OUP 1938)

The New Leviathan – R.G. Collingwood (OUP 1942)

Chapter 8

In the Trojan Ditch: Collected Poems and Selected Translations – C.H. Sisson (Carcanet 1974)

Collected Poems – C.H. Sisson (Carcanet 1984)

Poems Selected – C.H. Sisson (Carcanet 1995)

God Bless Karl Marx! – Poems – C.H. Sisson (Carcanet 1987)

Antidotes: Poems – C.H. Sisson (Carcanet 1991)

What and Who: Poems – C.H. Sisson (Carcanet 1994)

Sixteen Sonnets – C.H. Sisson (Carcanet 1990)

The Divine Comedy: A New Verse Translation – C.H. Sisson (Carcanet 1980)

English Poetry 1900–1950: An Assessment – C.H. Sisson (Rupert Hart-Davis 1971)

Is there a Church of England? – C.H. Sisson (Carcanet 1993)

The Avoidance of Literature: Collected Essays – C.H. Sisson (Carcanet 1978)

Anglican Essays – C.H. Sisson (Carcanet 1983)

English Perspectives: Essays on Liberty and Government – C.H. Sisson (Carcanet 1992)

The Spirit of Public Administration – C.H. Sisson (Methuen 1959)

On The Lookout: A Partial Autobiography – C.H. Sisson (Carcanet 1989)

Christopher Homm: A novel – C.H. Sisson (Methuen 1965)